Finding Your Career in Human Services

Finding Your Career in Human Services

Shoshana D. Kerewsky

University of Oregon

Bassim Hamadeh, CEO and Publisher
Amy Smith, Project Editor
Christian Berk, Associate Production Editor
Emely Villavicencio, Senior Graphic Designer
Sara Schennum, Licensing Associate
Natalie Piccotti, Senior Marketing Manager
Kassie Graves, Vice President of Editorial
Jamie Giganti, Director of Academic Publishing

ISBN: 978-1-5165-3271-1 (pbk) / 978-1-5165-3272-8 (br)

Brief Contents

Preface   *xiii*

Acknowledgments   *xv*

Chapter 1 Your Career in Human Services   1

Chapter 2 Know Yourself   19

Chapter 3 Be Strategic   39

Chapter 4 Career Areas and Roles in Human Services   59

Chapter 5 Interviews With Human Services Students and
            Professionals   69

Chapter 6 Your Job Search   91

Chapter 7 Preparing for the Future of Human Services   121

Appendix A National Organization for Human Services (NOHS)   127

Appendix B NOHS *Ethical Standards for Human Services
            Professionals* (2015)   129

Appendix C Center for Credentialing and Education Human
            Services–Board Certified Practitioner Certificate   135

Appendix D CCE *HS-BCP Code of Ethics* (2009)   137

Appendix E National Association of Social Workers (NASW)   141

Appendix F NASW Code of Ethics (2017)   143

Appendix G NAADAC   145

Appendix H NAADAC/NCC AP *Code of Ethics* (2016)   147

Appendix I Online Career and Self-Knowledge
            Tests and Tools   149

References   *151*

Index   *159*

About the Author   *163*

Detailed Contents

Preface   *xiii*

Acknowledgments   *xv*

Chapter 1
Your Career in Human Services   1

What is Human Services?   1

A Brief Historical Overview of Contemporary Human Services   1

Human Services Occupations   2

Human Services and Related Undergraduate Degrees   2

Career Outlook   3

Why Choose Human Services?   3

Some Practical Considerations   3

Human Diversity and Multiculturalism   5

Ethics in Human Services   6

The Human Services Scope of Practice   6

The Relationship Between Laws and Ethics   6

Ethical Requirements of Agencies, Academic Programs,
and Professional Organizations   6

Differences Between Professional Ethics Codes   7

The Structure of Professional Ethics Codes   7

The Importance of Professional Ethics   9

Your Faculty and Trainers' Gatekeeping Role   9

Supervision   11

Human Services Knowledge and Skills   12

Example: The Basic Listening Sequence (BLS)   12

Evaluating Your Career Strengths and Areas of Competence,
Part 1   13

Your Career Center   13

Career Familiarity and General Occupation Descriptions   14

O*NET Resources   14

Occupational Outlook Handbook (OOH)   15

Career Interest, Skills, and Other Tests   15

Self-Directed Search (SDS)   16

Additional Online Resources   17
Additional Campus Resources   18
Looking Ahead   18

Chapter 2
Know Yourself   19

You're Human, Too!   19
Reasons for Entering a Human Services Career   19
Tools for Career Self-Evaluation   20
   Activities for Informal Exploration   20
   Hays's ADDRESSING Framework   20
   Kliman's Social Matrix   22
   The Genogram   22
   The Johari Window   23
   Bronfenbrenner's Ecological Model   24
Evaluating Your Career Strengths and Areas of Competence, Part 2 26
   Career Counseling for Self-Exploration   26
   Myers-Briggs Type Indicator® (MBTI®)   26
   FIRO-B®   29
   Big Five Personality Test   30
   Free Online Career and Preference Tests   30
   Other Career and Vocational Assessments   30
Understanding Your Triggers and Vulnerabilities   31
Transference, Countertransference, and Ethical Practice   31
Self-Care and Avoiding Burnout   34
Using Self-Help, Counseling, and Other Interventions   36
Questions for Career Self-Reflection   36

Chapter 3
Be Strategic   39

Why Strategize?   39
Utilize Your Program and Institutional Resources   39

Your Program Handbook   39
Program Accreditation   40
"Informed Consent for Being a Student"   40
Classes and Other Requirements   41
Special Graduation Requirements   41
Policies Related to Good Standing and Problem Areas   41
Resources for Students   42
"Informed Consent for Students" Is an Ongoing Process   42
Academic Advisors   42
Program Website and Institutional Resources   43
Peers   44
Present Yourself Professionally   45
A Note to First-Generation College Students   45
Getting the Most From Your Site Placements   45
Site Placement Basics   46
Be Strategic About Your Field Placements   47
Other Site Considerations   50
Using Site Placements to Explore the Field   51
Supervisors, Faculty, Staff, and Fellow Students Are Site Resources   52
Other Opportunities to Explore the Field   53
Finding More Placement Opportunities   53
Service-Learning Experiences   53
Noncredit Experiences   53
What to Do Now   54
Professional Organizations and Conferences   54
Cultivate Relationships With Faculty, Staff, Supervisors,
Peers, Alumni/ae, and Students   55
Engage Fully and Challenge Yourself With Your Classes and
Site Placements   55
Look at Employment Ads   55
Identify and Reduce Potential Obstacles   56
Groom Your Public Presence   56
Start or Update Your Professional Portfolio   56
Be Flexible   58

Chapter 4
Career Areas and Roles in Human Services   59

Career Options in Human Services   59
Career Development   59
Using Your Holland (RIASEC) Code and Other Career Tests
to Think About Your Career Development   61

Direct Service   61
   Typical Characteristics of Direct Service Providers   62
   Direct Service Roles   62
Indirect Service   64
   Typical Characteristics of Indirect Service Providers   64
   Indirect Service Roles   65
Specialized Roles   65
   Research   65
   International Positions   66
   Related Positions   66
Other Considerations   66
Real People, Real Jobs   68

Chapter 5
Interviews With Human Services Students and Professionals   69

Career Trajectories in Human Services   69
   Moira: A Current Human Services Student   69
   Diane: A Community College Certificate Holder
   and Community Mental Health Provider   71
   Akiko: A Recent Human Services Graduate Working in a Nonprofit Agency   73
   Jade: Peace Corps Volunteer in Perú   75
   Niki: From Nontraditional Student to Varied Human Services
   and Educational Practice   76
   Rachel: From Human Services to Research
   and a Future PhD in Counseling Psychology   80
   David Gardiepy: Program Coordinator of a Training
   and Education Organization   82
   Bhavia Wagner: Building an International Organization From Scratch   84
Thinking about Human Services: The Interviews and Beyond   87
Common and Differing Elements of the Interviews   89

Chapter 6
Your Job Search   91

Resources for Your Job Search   91
   Finding Jobs   91
   Finding Job Announcements   92
Put Yourself Out There!   92
   Promoting Yourself through Professional Behavior   92
   Trainings and Conferences   94
   Membership in Professional Organizations   95

Posting Your Credentials Online 95
Preparing Your Materials 96
Resume and Curriculum Vitae (CV, or Vita) Options 96
Resume and CV Templates 96
Resumes 97
Utility of the Resume 97
Resume Tips 98
CVs 98
Resume vs. CV 98
Save a Master Copy! 99
Tips for Resume and CV Writing 100
Track Everything! 100
Your Email Address 100
Format and Describe Consistently 100
Tailor Your Resume or CV to the Job Announcement 101
Use the Announcement's Terminology 101
Protect Client Confidentiality in Descriptions of Previous Work 102
Be Accurate and Honest 102
Other Uses for Your CV 102
Cover Letters 103
Don't Be Negative 103
Keep Your Format Simple and Clean 103
Account for Gaps and Problem Areas 103
Professional Wording for Self-Disclosures 103
Promoting Yourself in Your Cover Letter 104
Describe What the Job Offers You 104
Resources for Preparing Your Resume/CV and Cover Letter 104
Additional Materials 105
Your Professional Portfolio 105
Use New Rather Than Standing Reference Letters 106
Sending Your Application 106
Interviews 106
Before You Get the Call 107
Telephone and Voice Mail Considerations 107
Online Considerations 107
Preparing for the Interview 107
Review Your Materials 107
Write Questions 107
Notes 108
Professional Attire 108
The Interview 108
Organizing Yourself 108

Interview Questions | *109*
Every Aspect of Your Interaction With the Site Is Part of Your Interview | *109*
Stay Positive | *110*
Don't Forget to Ask Your Questions About the Position | *110*
Activities to Prepare Yourself for Your Job Search | 112
Construct Your Resume and CV | *112*
Before You Interview | *112*
Reengage in Values Clarification | 113
Stepping Stones vs. Your Dream Job | 113
Licensure, Certification, and Similar Credentialing | 115
Associate's- and Bachelor's-Level Licensure and Certification | *116*
Managing a Felony Conviction | *116*
Licensing Requirements | *116*
Certification Requirements | *116*
The Qualified Mental Health Associate (QMHA) and Other Designations | *117*
Graduate School | 118
Tips for Avoiding Common Job Application Errors and Problems | 118
What to Do If You Can't Get a Job | 119

Chapter 7
Preparing for the Future of Human Services 121

Living in the Future | 121
The Impact of Technology | 123
The Impact of Cultural Change | 123
New Times, New Occupations | 124
Human Services Is a Job Growth Area | 124
You Change, Too! | 124

Appendix A National Organization for Human Services (NOHS) | 127

Appendix B NOHS *Ethical Standards for Human Services Professionals* (2015) | 129

Appendix C Center for Credentialing and Education Human Services—Board Certified Practitioner Certificate | 135

Appendix D CCE *HS–BCP Code of Ethics* (2009) | 137

Appendix E National Association of Social Workers (NASW) | 141

Appendix F NASW Code of Ethics (2017) | 143

Appendix G NAADAC   145

Appendix H NAADAC/NCC AP *Code of Ethics* **(2016)**   147

Appendix I
Online Career and Self-Knowledge Tests and Tools   149

    Consolidated Sites   149
    Test-Specific Sites   149

References   *151*
Index   *159*
About the Author   *163*

Preface

Finding Your Career in Human Services is intended as a starting point for students majoring, minoring, or with an interest in human services and related areas of study who are enrolled in certificate programs, community colleges, 4-year colleges, and universities. Much of the content is also applicable to human services graduates and those with similar majors who are engaged in a job search. It emphasizes opportunities and resources for career knowledge development and skills enhancement during your college education, and incorporates topics such as professional ethics, human diversity, frequent motivations for entering the human services field, and more.

This text covers approaches to your job search, resources, and potential areas of future growth. It is intended to be read in order, but you may find that some chapters apply more to your life and circumstances than others. It identifies important considerations for students who may not be aware of or engaged in career exploration and professional development, as well as those who are more advanced in these processes.

Chapter 1: Your Career in Human Services provides background and some basics on the human services professions, and introduces your career center resources, including some common career tests that can help you find jobs that are a good match for your interests.

Chapter 2: Know Yourself explores reasons people enter the field and provides both tools for self-evaluation and more career tests. It also discusses triggers and vulnerabilities that can decrease competence and job satisfaction, with suggested resources for addressing these issues.

Chapter 3: Be Strategic is best suited for current or future human services students. It describes typical features of academic human services programs that can serve as resources for your career exploration and job search. It also describes opportunities for your career development through your field site placements and professional organizations. It introduces some of the job search tools you will use and materials you will develop in Chapter 6.

Chapter 4: Career Areas and Roles in Human Services delves deeper into career development and interpersonal characteristics of human services occupations.

Chapter 5: Interviews with Human Services Professionals includes interviews with eight human services students and professionals, as well as activities to clarify your job preferences.

Chapter 6: Your Job Search presents resources for job hunting; tips for promoting yourself, making contacts, and developing your written materials; and interview advice. It also explores your decision-making about ideal, adequate, and survival jobs, and explains some options for enhancing your job qualifications.

Chapter 7: Preparing for the Future of Human Services points to growth in the human services field, as well as human services jobs that have only recently come into existence.

The appendices include information on several relevant professional organizations and their ethics codes. Also included is a list of the online career and self-knowledge tests and tools described in Chapters 1 and 2.

This book is based on 18 years as a faculty member in the Counseling Psychology and Human Services Department of University of Oregon and over 30 years of counseling, teaching, and advising community college and university undergraduates about their professional development. I hope it is useful for your career explorations. May your career in human services bring you as much pleasure as mine has.

Shoshana D. Kerewsky, PsyD, HS-BCP
Eugene, Oregon

Acknowledgments

My heartfelt thanks are due to Dr. Krista M. Chronister, who was my student and career coach long before she became my colleague and associate dean. Thanks also to Dr. Lauren Lindstrom, Dr. Tammi Dice, Dr. Gigi Franyo-Ehlers, Dr. Cara DiMarco, and my colleagues at the University of Oregon College of Education and in NOHS leadership for your guidance and many acts of personal and professional kindness. My students and colleagues in the Women in Transition program at Lane Community College provided valuable insights on career development, as have my undergraduate and graduate students in the Counseling Psychology and Human Services Department. The human services students and professionals who allowed me to interview them for this book graciously shared their time and experiences in order to help the future colleagues who read their stories. That's human services in action!

Kassie Graves, my Cognella editor, has been a steady and reassuring presence during the writing of this book.

As always, my greatest appreciation and affection belong to Dr. Nancy Taylor Kemp, who has served as my sounding board and taken on additional responsibilities that were properly mine so that I would be free to write.

Chapter 1

Your Career in Human Services

What is Human Services?

Human services is the umbrella term covering a variety of professional and paraprofessional activities that provide helping services to people and communities. The National Organization for Human Services (NOHS), the largest professional organization for human services students, professionals, and faculty, defines the field as

> meeting human needs through an interdisciplinary knowledge base, focusing on prevention as well as remediation of problems, and maintaining a commitment to improving the overall quality of life of service populations. The Human Services profession is one which promotes improved service delivery systems by addressing not only the quality of direct services, but also by seeking to improve accessibility, accountability, and coordination among professionals and agencies in service delivery. (*NOHS, n.d.*)

NOHS goes on to say that "the primary purpose of the human services professional is to assist individual and communities to function as effectively as possible in the major domains of living" (NOHS, n.d.). This broad definition encompasses jobs as diverse as nanny, case manager, addictions interventionist, coach, nursing home enrichment specialist, community organizer, human resources officer, parole officer, medical assistant, researcher, resident director, home care assistant, grant writer, special needs classroom assistant, EMT, and psychiatrist.

A Brief Historical Overview of Contemporary Human Services

Compared to specific human services fields, such as social work and counseling, the general field of human services has a shorter history with roots in cultural changes that fostered services intended to keep vulnerable people in their communities rather than in residential institutions. This period of deinstitutionalization and community care led to a blossoming of the human services field. At that time, some of the roles that today are performed by human services graduates were held by paraprofessionals (volunteers or front-line employees who were skilled but not formally qualified through academic programs or professional credentialing). In 1956, the first associate's program in mental health was established (Quinsigamond Community College, 2018).

At the same time as large residential institutions decreased and community-based services increased, changes occurred that increased sources of funding for human services. For example, Medicare was created in 1965, and CHIP (Children's Health Insurance Program) became available in 1997 (Parsons, 2015). The Affordable Care Act (ACA) was signed by President Obama in 2010 (eHealth, 2018). Current discussions about the scope and rules of the ACA are a good example of why funding for human services fluctuates, and therefore the number and types of human services jobs available, as well as salary rates.

Human Services Occupations

Generalist human services degrees at the associate's and bachelor's level typically teach the skills and competencies needed in order to be effective in a wide variety of direct and indirect service occupations at the entry level and higher. Some jobs within human services, such as psychotherapist, require additional training, education, and credentialing or licensure.

Recognition of the generalist human services field continues to grow, and undergraduate human services professionals find work in ever more diverse areas of service provision. For example, it is increasingly common to find human services professionals providing skills training, behavioral support, and intakes in primary care medical settings.

The typical activities and roles of associate's- and bachelor's-level human services professionals are described later in this book. A human services degree prepares you for many kinds of work within the human services field as well as elsewhere.

Human services professionals work at social service agencies, resource centers, mental health facilities, schools, medical clinics, residential addictions treatment centers, hospitals, nonprofit agencies, large organizations and corporations, government offices and facilities, commissions, and many others. This book uses the term *agency* as shorthand for the varied job settings where human services graduates find work.

The Bureau of Labor Statistics (BLS) (2011) provides a 12-page brochure that goes into some detail about the roles and job responsibilities of human services professionals, as well as typical human services settings and client populations served.

Human Services and Related Undergraduate Degrees

Associate's and bachelor's degree programs in human services are increasingly available. These may be generalist programs, or they may have a specific focus, such as chemical dependency. They may include opportunities to earn an academic certificate in an area of practice, such as gerontology or HIV/AIDS. You may also have the option to minor in human services.

Some schools offer degrees in social work (BSW), psychology, human development, early childhood education, criminal justice, social welfare, or similar majors. These programs may be similar to and overlap with generalist human services programs, but they have their own histories and areas of emphasis. Depending on your course of study and number of supervised field or service-learning placements, these majors may qualify you for some jobs and certifications in the generalist human services arena. Even degrees like sociology or pre-nursing may meet some requirements and help you to be competitive in the field.

Training programs emphasize competencies, professional ethics and conduct, relevant theory, and supervised practice. They qualify you for professional roles that require applied skills and qualifications. Paraprofessional jobs are also available; these tend to require less education, have fewer and less sensitive responsibilities, and require ongoing supervision or management from a professional.

Even if you are early in your human services program or are in a different but related major, every human services-related class improves your qualifications for a satisfying job in the field.

Career Outlook

The broad human services field has been robust and continues to grow. The Bureau of Labor Statistics tracks overall U.S. employment trends (BLS, 2018a). At the time of this writing, the U.S. economy was doing well and workers were needed in many fields (Irwin, 2018). The BLS employment projections include many human services professions among the fastest growing occupations currently and projected through 2026 (BLS, 2018b).

Why Choose Human Services?

Students choose a human services career for many different reasons. Typically, students have previous paraprofessional experience in human services or related roles, enjoy working with people or in the systems that support direct services, and have received feedback that they are good at this work. Chapter 2 goes into more depth about personal motivations for entering the field, as well as providing activities that help you describe yourself and some preference tests and instruments that focus on your personality and interpersonal style in the world of work. The present chapter introduces some of the career tests and instruments that can help you find emphasis areas and specific jobs and determine whether they are a good fit for your interests, skills, and future abilities.

Some Practical Considerations

Before looking at career instruments and job-finding tools, it is important to mention some practical considerations associated with the choice of a human services career. The first consideration is your educational expenses. If you are not yet enrolled in a human services program, or are early in your college experience, you may or may not have thought about the relative costs of a community college degree versus a 4-year college or university degree. You may want to look at some job listings using the resources in this chapter and Chapter 6 to see if jobs that interest you require a 4-year degree. If not, shorter community college programs may be more economical. You may also want to speak with a financial aid advisor, career counselor, or academic advisor to learn about scholarships or sources of funding for which you might qualify.

The second consideration is the importance the human services professions place on self-knowledge and, at times, self-disclosure to your supervisors or instructors. If you do not enjoy examining your motives or working to understand how your past history, beliefs, and attitudes influence the services you provide to vulnerable populations, you may find a human services program challenging. Your academic advisor may be able to

Side Box 1.1

Why Human Services for Me?

To begin your career exploration, ask yourself these questions. You may want to write down or discuss your answers with a classmate. You can also interview each other and expand on these questions for a deeper understanding of your motivations for entering this field. Return to your answers after reading Chapters 1 and 2 to see if you want to add additional thoughts.

- How do I define human services?
- How did I first learn about my major? About the field?
- What events and experiences in my own life help make the idea of working in human services attractive? What events in my family's and friends' lives and my community contribute to the idea of working in this field?
- Which of my skills are likely to contribute to my career in human services? Which of my personal characteristics?
- Which types of human services jobs and populations appeal to me?
- What excites me about the field?
- What are my other life passions and goals? How do they integrate with human services?
- What are my reservations about entering this field? About particular types of human services jobs?
- What are my resources for learning more or resolving these concerns?

point you toward related majors or program tracks that require less exploration of your own history and behavior.

Human Diversity and Multiculturalism

Another factor to consider is human diversity and culture. Everyone, including clients and human services professionals, has many identities. Your human services education will include learning to work effectively with people who are different from you, and with people you may share group memberships with but who may nonetheless have different identities and needs. Proficiency in interacting with and providing services to diverse populations is increasingly emphasized in human services programs.

Some students see themselves as not being diverse, as "being boring," or as having no culture. It is sometimes difficult to see your own group identities and culture if you are in the majority or do not have very much exposure to people who are different from you. Chapter 2 provides some tools for noticing and understanding your own diversity and providing you and your trainers with some context for your work in human services.

You may want to start with the exercise Circles of My Multicultural Self (Gorski, 1995–2015) (Figure 1.1). This simple activity is a good starting point for exploring your identities. Write your name in the central circle in the diagram. In each of the four smaller circles, write one of your important identities. These can include descriptions such as ethnicity, education, sexual orientation, gender, religion, or veteran's status; and roles such as brother, crisis line worker, skier, or other identities that are important to you. You can add more circles if you want to. Gorski's worksheet and the website listed in the references include activities and questions that you can explore on your own or talk over with a friend or classmate. For the purposes of this book, you may want to answer the question, "How do my identities relate to my future career in human services?"

Understanding your own group memberships, beliefs, and practices contributes to your multicultural and diversity competence and decreases your countertransference (see Chapter 2).

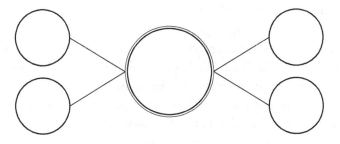

FIGURE 1.1   Circles of My Multicultural Self.

Ethics in Human Services

The Human Services Scope of Practice

Human services is a professional field with its own ethical standards, as well as laws that control what you are allowed to do (depending on your qualifications) and what the agency or organization you work for is allowed to do. This is called your *scope of practice*. For example, a person with a bachelor's degree in human services may be permitted to provide behavioral support services, but not counseling or psychotherapy. It is important to know the laws governing your professional activities, and this is not consistent across state lines. Ask your field site supervisor to review the relevant laws and explain the processes you are to follow as a student. Although many students initially think that ethics are clear cut and obvious, this frequently is not the case. If you make use of your ethics experts while you are a student, you will be much better prepared for complicated, messy situations you encounter as a professional.

The Relationship Between Laws and Ethics

Law and ethics are not the same thing, but they often refer to each other and sometimes overlap. Sometimes they do not, which can pose an ethical dilemma. For example, human services ethics codes normally discuss *confidentiality* (the technical term for certain aspects of client privacy), but may not explain the limits of confidentiality in much detail. However, your state law may require you to breach confidentiality under some conditions, such as when someone is harming a child or elder. Use your faculty and supervisors to help you anticipate areas where your state laws and your professional ethics are in conflict, and learn what steps you can take to decrease this discrepancy.

Advanced human services professions usually require a graduate degree, such as a master's of social work (MSW), and are likely to require that the professional be licensed in that state as well. (For more on licenses and certificates, see Chapter 6.) Sometimes, licensees are required to adhere to a specific code of ethics. For example, Oregon law requires licensed psychologists to follow the American Psychological Association's ethics code. However, sometimes licensees are not legally required to follow an ethics code, although they may need to follow similar guidelines, referred to as a *code of conduct*, that is embedded in the state licensing laws.

Ethical Requirements of Agencies, Academic Programs, and Professional Organizations

Some agencies and organizations require employees to follow a specific set of ethical standards. For example, a chemical dependency program may follow the NAADAC-NCC AP ethics code (see Appendix G and H). Ask whether the agencies where you are engaged in field placements require you to follow an ethics code.

Your academic program may require you to function under one or more ethics codes. This includes not just in your field site, but in the classroom and in the community. This is one reason that human services students are sometimes referred to as *professionals in training*—you are expected to act ethically even though you are not yet a qualified or credentialed professional.

In addition, joining a professional organization carries with it your agreement to follow that organization's ethical standards. This includes student memberships, even though the codes are written as if you are a qualified professional, so some parts may not be relevant to you until you graduate. Becoming a member or student member of a professional organization demonstrates that you are willing to hold yourself to a set of ethical standards.

The major professional organization for human services students and professionals is the National Organization for Human Services (NOHS) (2018). You will find more information about NOHS in Appendix A and the NOHS ethical standards in Appendix B. Students earning a bachelor's degree in social work (BSW) typically will be required to follow the ethics of the National Association of Social Workers (NASW) (2018a). Information about NASW is in Appendix A, and an overview of the NASW ethics code is in Appendix B. Psychology students may be in programs that follow the American Psychological Association's (APA) (2017) or the American Counseling Association's (ACA) (2014) ethical standards.

Human services professionals who receive the national Human Services-Board Certified Practitioner (HS-BCP) credential (Center for Credentialing and Education, 2016a) must follow the ethical standards for HS-BCPs (CCE, 2009). Information about the HS-BCP certification is in Appendix C and an overview of the ethics code is in Appendix D.

As you can imagine, behaving ethically and resolving conflicts between the law and your ethical standards, or between two ethics codes (such as being a NOHS member in an agency operating under NAADAC ethics) can be complex. Your ethics instructor and your field site supervisor can help you untangle these difficult situations.

Differences Between Professional Ethics Codes

While human services ethics codes may look similar and cover similar topics, they differ in ways that demonstrate important aspects of each profession's culture. For example, there are differences between the ways the ethics codes of NOHS, NASW, and APA set limits on certain kinds of multiple-role relationships (for example, having a professional relationship with a client, and also having an additional relationship with that client in the community). These differences reflect the different scopes of practice for human services professionals, social workers, and psychologists. They also convey each profession's understanding of the client role and client vulnerabilities. Social work, which has the most stringent standards for multiple-role relationships, sees any past or present client as a potential future client, so it limits certain kinds of relationships that are permitted in some of the other human services professional codes (Stephen Behnke, personal communication).

The Structure of Professional Ethics Codes

Most human services ethics codes include aspirational principles, which are not enforceable but describe more abstract goals for your professional conduct, such as advocacy, social justice, respect for all clients, diversity and multicultural competence, and others. Take

The Most Important Ethical Standards, According to Site Supervisors

No matter which ethics code(s) you follow, some common ethical standards are likely to be emphasized early in your academic program. When I teach the human services ethics class at my university, I always ask several of the field site supervisors which ethical standards they want to be sure I discuss with our students in the very first week. They consistently give these answers:

- Client welfare: This is considered the most important ethical standard, because it encompasses all of the other standards and obligations associated with human services work. Human services students and professionals put client welfare first and remain highly aware of their responsibilities to the vulnerable people and communities they serve.

- Confidentiality: The kinds of privacy to which clients and student-clients are entitled, what to do if you meet your client outside the agency, ways to discuss client issues in order to receive supervision on site and in your campus supervision or practicum class.

- Multiple-role relationships: Recognizing possible multiple-role relationships, decreasing the likelihood of entering into problematic multiple-role relationships, safeguarding client confidentiality if a nonproblematic multiple-role relationship cannot be avoided, what to do if someone you know comes to your agency for services.

- Competence: Understanding that you are a trainee and that your supervisor is legally responsible for your actions (see below), asking for help, being able to articulate accurately what you know and don't know. Another aspect of competence is behaving professionally at the agency and in the community, and seeking help for personal issues that may affect your work with clients, such as a problem with substance use.

Look at the NOHS ethical standards in Appendix B to see how each of these topics is described and how each relates to other ethical considerations.

a look at one or more of the human services ethics codes and see how well your personal and professional values match its aspirational principles.

Ethics codes also include guidelines for the most common needs and issues encountered by practitioners of that profession. Notice that some of the human services ethics codes include standards for topics such as teaching, conducting research, or administering psychological tests, while others do not. This can also give you insight into the activities of each profession.

The Importance of Professional Ethics

In summary, human services students and professionals are required to behave ethically, so ethics is an important part of your human services career. When you apply for jobs, it is very likely that you will be asked to respond to a case vignette that includes ethical considerations. You may also be asked how you responded to a professional ethical dilemma. Job applications, as well as applications for licensure, certification, credentialing renewals, professional liability insurance, and membership in professional organizations, typically ask about any legal or ethical violations you have been charged with or found to have committed. If you have any, you will need to explain them, and you may or may not have your application accepted.

Many people who would like to enter human services fields are unaware of the importance of professional ethics, not just for practicing professionals but also for students. Some academic programs and some field sites will not or cannot accept trainees who have engaged in serious legal or ethical violations. As described in Chapter 3, criminal background checks are often required by programs and sites. Under no circumstances should you misrepresent or omit information in answer to ethical and legal questions in background check, academic, field placement, job, liability insurance, professional membership, or credentialing applications or renewals. Doing so is at best dishonest, unethical, and illegal. At worst, it is a felony, or may entirely bar you from working in human services. If you are unsure how to describe previous legal and ethical violations you have committed, talk with an academic advisor in the major, or a campus student legal advisor, to learn about how to document them, potential restrictions on academic training program entry or community placements, and how to address these issues when you are asked about them.

Your Faculty and Trainers' Gatekeeping Role

Your faculty, staff, and supervisors, as well as your educational institution and field site, have legal and ethical responsibility for your actions. While you are in training, or when you are working under a supervisor in some job roles, you are functioning under their or the agency's license or certification. It may be helpful to think of the student role as if you are an extension—a hand or a set of computer subroutines—of your staff and supervisors. You have some autonomy, but your actions have consequences for the people above you. This is one of many good reasons to act as they direct you to, and to not act as they direct as well. If you don't understand or if you disagree with a directive, ask for clarification and raise your concerns. This is an important aspect of ethical behavior.

For all of these reasons, academic programs for applied human services fields have what is called a *gatekeeping* function. This means that while you are a student in the program, or are enrolled in service-learning or field study (practicum or internship) placements

A Typical Job Interview Case Vignette
That Includes Ethical Issues

As part of a job interview, you may be presented with and asked to respond to vignettes similar to this case, where some major ethics issues are clearly identified. Read the vignette and look at the NOHS ethics code in Appendix B. What ethical issues can you identify?

Bernard Gallo, AAS, is one of two case managers at Vinaville Social Services (VSS), the only human services agency in a rural town that is about 45 miles from the next community of any size. VSS keeps client records in an electronic database. All VSS employees have access to the client records. Except for VSS, there are only a few human services professionals in Vinaville—a master's level counselor who has an addictions certificate, a social worker who is in semi-retirement, and a family therapist who only works with couples. Bernard oversees the work of three paraprofessionals with high school diplomas or GEDs. These paraprofessionals conduct intake interviews and basic screenings for issues such as depression, anxiety, and suicidality, as well as a computerized symptom checklist that generates a report that lists possible psychiatric diagnoses. The paraprofessionals review the results and assign new clients to the case manager who has the most expertise with those issues and possible diagnoses. The case manager develops a client service plan and meets with the client periodically to ensure that the client is satisfied and that the services are still necessary. When Bernard logged into the client database this morning, he reviewed the intake information for a new client in his caseload. Because Vinaville is small, Bernard recognizes the client and knows that she is the sister of the paraprofessional who conducted her intake and screening.

If you were Bernard, what ethical issues would you identify in this situation? What steps could you have taken to decrease ethical issues before this situation arose? What steps can you take now to minimize or resolve the ethical issues?

Even if you are given a case vignette that doesn't appear to have ethical issues or an ethics focus, it will help you sort out the other issues if you identify the ethical underpinnings of the situation, or places where the professionals are acting ethically. This will make your answer more comprehensive and demonstrate your awareness of ethical standards (which is attractive to employers).

even before entering the major, or as part of the admissions process for programs with this requirement, faculty and staff are responsible for evaluating you in many ways. This includes not only whether you are a good academic fit for the program, but also if you are, and continue to be, a good ethical fit. Input from your field site supervisors provides important feedback on your ethics while you are at your site, which is the training component most similar to the work you will perform as a graduated human services professional. Your site behaviors include the standard of competent practice. Examples may be actions like dressing at the site's professional standard (which could mean jeans and a tee shirt at some sites, but never a tee shirt with a beer bottle or obscenities on it), arriving on time, giving timely notice when you are ill or cannot make it to your placement, responding to your supervisor and other staff, receiving feedback appropriately, presenting yourself in a way that does not make clients distrust the profession or agency, and similar aspects of your comportment as a trainee. In other words, even from your program application or first encounter with the academic program or your field placement sites, the human services professionals responsible for your training and actions are evaluating your goodness of fit for the profession (Lichtenstein, Lindstrom, & Kerewsky, 2005; Kerewsky, 2016).

On the bright side, most students act in accordance with their program's and school's conduct and other standards (and handbook, if available), ask for clarification when they need it, think and act like professionals in training, adhere to their jurisdiction's legal requirements, and follow their ethical standards. If you do, too, you will minimize the risk of not being admitted or not obtaining a field site, being put on a remediation plan, or even being removed from your program. You will have the satisfaction of knowing that your attention and scrupulousness result in a higher quality of care for your clients, and demonstrate that you belong in this field!

Supervision

Supervision is an important aspect of training and managing ethical, competent human services professionals. The term can refer to a number of different relationships. Several that are most common in human services include the following:

+ Campus supervisor: Associated with your academic program, this person may teach your practicum or field study class or coordinate with your field site supervisor. Typically, the person on campus who is above you in a hierarchy and has legal and ethical responsibility for your actions. This person may also be responsible for your welfare as a student, although this is generally shared by all faculty and staff in your program.

+ Field site supervisor: Similar to your campus supervisor, the person at your site who has legal and ethical responsibility for your actions. You probably have a regular supervision meeting with this person, either individually or in a group, to receive feedback, support, and training. You may also be trained by or meet with staff members who are not your supervisor (but still have legal and ethical responsibilities related to your training). You may have more than one supervisor. Your field site supervisor typically provides feedback on your performance to you and your academic program.

- Job supervisor: Someone who has managerial responsibility for you and oversees your work, but who is not necessarily legally responsible for your actions if you are not a trainee.

If you are not sure who your supervisors are on campus and at your field site, don't hesitate to ask.

Human Services Knowledge and Skills

Everything you learn in your human services education and training is useful for your career exploration and job search. At a very basic and practical level, every course and every placement you complete successfully is a job qualification that demonstrates your acquisition and use of professional knowledge and skills. In addition, some of your new learning may help you directly with your job search.

Example: The Basic Listening Sequence (BLS)

As just one example, a student who takes a class on interpersonal or interviewing skills may receive training in using the Basic Listening Sequence portion of the Microskills Pyramid (Ivey, Ivey, & Zalaquett, 2018).

The BLS is a versatile tool for reminding yourself to use active listening and specific forms of interpersonal engagement when you are being interviewed, just as you would use these skills in a clinical setting. Your use of the BLS also demonstrates your interpersonal skillfulness to the person evaluating you for a job.

Side Box 1.4

The Basic Listening Sequence (BLS)

Ivey, Ivey, and Zalaquett's Basic Listening Sequence (BLS) is a hierarchy of interpersonal skills built on a base of "ethics, multicultural competence, neuroscience, and positive psychology/resilience" (p. 12). In order of increasing complexity and incorporating the previous components, the elements of the BLS are:

- Attending and Empathy Skills
- Observation Skills
- Questions
- Encouraging, Paraphrasing, and Summarizing
- Reflecting Feelings

How could you utilize the BLS when you are an applicant for a job?

Using the BLS in a job interview is one example of how your human services education results in transferrable skills. Don't forget to bring all of your professional learning to your career exploration and job search!

Evaluating Your Career Strengths and Areas of Competence, Part 1

Your Career Center

Although it is possible simply to graduate from your school, call an agency, and apply for a job, you are more likely to be successful if you are more systematic and engage in the activities described in this book. You have many resources for your career search, and a career center is an efficient place to start.

Your school may have a career center (either free-standing or through a general counseling and advising office). You may also be able to use career counseling resources at your local community college, university, or government employment office. If your school does not have a career center and there are none nearby that you can get permission to use, you will still be able to gather information and develop your materials, but you will not have individualized guidance. You may want to gather a career exploration and planning group with your classmates so you can share ideas and strategies. All of the online career and preference tests and instruments described in this chapter and Chapter 2 are listed in Appendix I.

Career centers typically offer a counselor or advisor with whom you can discuss your career search. Career counselors can help you learn about your job skills and preferences, identify related jobs with which you may not be familiar, and provide resources for your job search. These may include additional internships, job listings, job fair information, personal contacts with graduates or other people in that career. They may also direct you to career biographies that describe different jobs, associate them with the results of different career tests, and provide accounts by people who have and love that job. The counselor may suggest resources in the center and online. Many tools that help you explore your preferences and options are available at career centers, either free or for a fee. This may be less expensive than using them online on your own.

Career centers may also provide resume, CV, and cover letter workshops or assistance; interview practice; and other forms of job coaching. They will know when the next job fair is scheduled, how to contact a Peace Corps representative, where your local military recruiting offices are, and other important information. Students with felony convictions or other limiting factors can receive guidance from a career counselor, who can point you in productive directions and steer you away from occupations that may not be willing to consider your job application.

Another advantage of meeting with someone at the career center is that that person can oversee, score, and interpret your results, integrating them with an interview or other results in order to discuss your unique career preferences and options.

Career Familiarity and General Occupation Descriptions

Before taking career tests and reviewing your results, it is useful to become familiar with some of the most efficient and common general career exploration and job-finding resources. Many of these sources of information are governmental and help you to learn about jobs and groups of related jobs in and of themselves. This activity is distinct from your targeted job search, which uses different resources and is described in Chapter 6. Fortunately, the tools from the U.S. Bureau of Labor Statistics (BLS) and O*NET Online, as well as other sources, are available online free of charge. You can preview them before meeting with a career counselor or academic advisor, or use them to guide your individual exploration.

If you are not familiar with the specialized vocabulary used in human services professions, take a look at the *Dictionary of Counseling & Human Services: An Essential Resource for Students and Professional Helpers* (Neukrug, Kalkbrenner, & Snow, 2017).

O*NET Resources

A good place to start is O*NET (National Center for O*NET Development, 2018), especially if you are new to human services or unfamiliar with the range of occupations in the field. O*NET is a general career resource where you can look up a particular job or use codes from elsewhere on the site as well as other crosswalk strategies to find clustered occupations that are similar to each other.

O*NET has pages for veterans, Spanish-language links, and shortcuts for searching the site by codes from the Occupational Outlook Handbook (OOH) described below (Bureau of Labor Statistics [BLS], 2018c).

If the site seems overwhelming, start with O*NET's Interest Profiler (National Center for O*NET Development, n.d.a), which asks about your interests and associates them with careers in order to guide your search. You can also use O*NET's Advanced Search function to do a skills search at https://www.onetonline.org/skills/ (National Center for O*NET Development, n.d.b). O*NET's skills lists fall under these categories:

- Basic Skills
- Complex Problem Solving Skills
- Resource Management Skills
- Social Skills
- Systems Skills
- Technical Skills

O*NET also has an advanced search option that lets you identify software with which you are familiar to generate a list of jobs that use this specific skill.

If you are not sure which of the skills you would like to use in a job, think about a hobby or avocation that you enjoy. Use the skills associated with your hobby to complete the skills search to learn about jobs that may require the same skills you use for fun. This is also a good strategy for veterans or others who are shifting careers because it changes your focus from the job skills you have (but which may lead you to a type of job you no longer want) to potentially transferable job skills (which may be unexpected or bring novelty and more pleasure to your work).

O*NET provides a different approach through its Work Values page (National Center for O*NET Development, n.d.c). You can click on any of these values to see jobs associated with them:

+ Achievement
+ Independence
+ Recognition
+ Relationships
+ Support
+ Working Conditions

Clicking any value link takes you to a screen where you can choose multiple values (for example, Achievement, Relationships, and Support). Choosing the ranking option of RSA brings up a number of human services occupations, including Personal Care Aides, Medical Assistants, Teacher Assistants, and Patient Representatives among others. The occupations marked with a sun symbol are Bright Outlook Occupations, meaning that many jobs are available or job growth is expected in the future. Follow the links to see a list of all Bright Outlook Occupations, or go directly to https://www.onetonline.org/help/bright/ (National Center for O*NET Development, n.d.d).

Every O*NET job title you click on takes you to a report on that profession. This includes typical job tasks, education required, work values, and much more data on this type of position.

Occupational Outlook Handbook (OOH)

The Bureau of Labor Statistics (BLS) website offers the extensive Occupational Outlook Handbook (OOH) (BLS, 2018c). The OOH is a compendium of most job titles and characteristics in the United States. Like O*NET, it includes job descriptions and job clusters. The clusters most relevant to a human services degree are Healthcare and Personal Care and Service. However, depending on your interests, jobs in other clusters may be a good fit for you as well. The OOH page includes tools to expand or narrow your search, including salary ranges and links to projected fastest growing occupations and highest new jobs projections. If you would like to read more about how to use the OOH, see Doyle (2018).

Career Interest, Skills, and Other Tests

Also available at your career center or online, career interest, skills, and other tests are instruments that help you to describe your interests and abilities in order to map these characteristics onto the descriptions of occupations covered in the previous section. Along with the self-exploratory activities and tools in Chapter 2, they provide you with a solid picture of yourself as a potential employee. They may also help you identify areas in which you will need more education and training in order to address knowledge and skills deficits or to explore your responses to the testing and the jobs associated with your results. If possible, it is best to work with a career counselor who can integrate your results and save you time by suggesting resources or other tests.

There is normally a fee to take these tests, but it may be lowered or waived by your career center. Free online instruments that claim they are similar to or based on these tests may or may not be valid and reliable, so if you take them, take them with a grain of salt.

Self-Directed Search (SDS)

The Self-Directed Search (SDS) (PAR, 2018a) is very commonly used and very helpful. If you can only take one career test, you should take the SDS because it is used with O*NET, the Occupational Outlook Handbook, and many other occupational databases.

The SDS asks questions about your work-related preferences and generates a Holland Code. This is a six-letter code (sometimes called the RIASEC code, which is an acronym for the first letters of the preference categories). It captures and ranks your work-related preferences in descending order. For example, someone highest in Social preferences and next-highest in Enterprising will see the "S" abbreviation appear first in her Holland Code, followed by the E. SDS provides you with a multipage report about your type and possible occupations that are likely to be a good fit for you.

The RIASEC categories, summarized very briefly from short descriptions at PAR's RIASEC Theory page (2018b), are below. Remember that these terms are being used as professional and technical language. You can be a realistic person without having a majority of Realistic preferences!

+ Realistic: Tend to prefer working with things, not people; often described as genuine, sensible, practical, natural, thrifty, modest, persistent, and honest.
+ Investigative: Tend to be logical and scientific, and prefer concepts and ideas more than working directly with people or things.
+ Artistic: Tend to prefer creative ideas; does not necessarily mean the person is an artist, but does indicate that he thinks about ideas in unconventional ways.
+ Social: Tend to prefer working with and helping people; many human services professions have "S" as their first Holland Code letter.
+ Enterprising: Tend to prefer working with concepts and people, and to be outgoing and interpersonally confident.
+ Conventional: Tend to prefer working with data and linear tasks; may enjoy working with numbers and databases; refers to the more traditional nature of the work; does not mean that you are conservative or formal.

PAR's RIASEC Theory page (2018b) also describes and provides a visual for the way your responses contribute to your Holland Code.

Your code is an especially valuable tool because once you obtain it, you can enter it directly into many career-related sites to bring up a list of jobs related to that type. The connection has been made by evaluating job responsibilities, as well as interviewing people who enjoy their jobs, and testing them to determine their Holland Codes. Therefore, when you look at the jobs associated with your Holland Code, there is a good chance that you may enjoy this occupation.

An extremely interesting site that brings the Holland Codes alive is VocBio: Vocational Biographies (n.d.). You can preview the site online, but to read the entries, you need to access the site through a career center or other subscriber, such as a public library. VocBio provides actual multiple-page stories of people who hold jobs with different Holland Codes. The stories include a typical day, the aspects of the job that the person likes and dislikes, the person's career trajectory, and photos. You can see additional Holland Code case studies at SDS Case Studies (PAR, 2018c).

Once you have taken the SDS or approximated your Holland Code, go to the general occupational websites and enter your code type to explore clusters and occupations that may be a good match for you.

Additional Online Resources

It is easy to be overwhelmed with resources and information, so be sure to narrow your search down in a way that works for you. Here are just a few of the many other online sites that consolidate links and information for career exploration. They are also listed by URL in Appendix I. Remember that online tests, quizzes, and instruments may not be valid or reliable, so always compare results with those of professional, research-based tools. Do not take quizzes or interest inventories on Facebook, because they frequently are phishing attempts or data skimming programs, not actual career services.

+ Assessment.com (n.d.): MAPP™ Career Assessment Test
+ The Balance Careers (n.d.): Career articles and tips

- Careeronestop (State of Minnesota, 2018): Many resources, organized more intuitively than some of the sites that present similar information and tools
- Monster Worldwide: 10 Awesome Free Career Self-Assessment Tools on the Internet (Conlan, 2018)
- The Muse: The 11 Best Career Quizzes to Help You Find Your Dream Job (The Muse Editor, 2018)
- MyPlan.com (2004–2018): Planning resources by academic cohort (e.g., college students or career changers); includes career data, lists, and other online resources; and links to assessment instruments, career values assessment, and other resources

Additional Campus Resources

If your educational institution offers career services or has a career center, you can visit on your own. You can also ask to have a career counselor or other qualified person visit a class or offer a program-wide workshop on career exploration and local resources. Even if your school does not offer career counseling, chances are that your faculty and advisors have connections to other programs and resources and can bring in guest speakers.

Looking Ahead

Chapter 2 describes more career instruments that focus on personal style, such as the Myers-Briggs Type Indicator® (MBTI®), the Big Five Personality Test, and FIRO-B®, which are often available through career centers.

Remember that codes, labels, and descriptors are characterizations. They are approximate and reflect your responses at a particular time and under particular circumstances. Although some personality traits are stable, many fluctuate. Career testing codes are a reflection of, not a limit on, what you can do if you want to.

Figure Credits

Know Yourself

You're Human, Too!

All of us interact with multiple systems that utilize the expertise and skills of human services personnel. These include physical and mental health care, local and national government, education, and many other systems that provide direct intervention, prevention services, enrichment opportunities, advocacy, research, and other activities that benefit the community directly and indirectly.

Reasons for Entering a Human Services Career

Students often enter human services professions for personal reasons. You and your family may have received helpful interventions and support from human services workers when you were a child. You may have had a medical issue, been adopted, been in a Head Start classroom, or participated in a sports program for at-risk youth. Your parent might have been in an anger management group or received emergency financial assistance during a crisis. Or maybe you received services as an adult, wrestling with your own problems or seeking support for your own children. These resources may have made a profound positive difference in your life, inspiring you to want to help others.

It's also possible that this human services safety net was not effective for you and your family. Resources you wanted or needed may not have been available, or not quite the right fit. Sadly, you may have experienced inadequate, ineffective, or even harmful interventions. In this case, your motivation to become a human services professional may include your wish to improve a system that failed you.

Whatever your reasons for entering the broad field of human services, it is important to engage in ongoing exploration of yourself, your choices about training opportunities and specific jobs, and how engaging in this work affects you. Being aware of your own strengths and vulnerabilities, in general and in relation to your career, will help you be a more ethical, competent, helpful, and satisfied professional. Learning more about your own strengths and limitations decreases the possibility of unintentionally harming your clients. Taking care of yourself is good ethical and clinical behavior, as well as great modeling for your clients and colleagues!

This chapter provides you with several tools for self-evaluation that may be useful for your career search, as well as a description of some more formal instruments that provide career and aptitude information. We then return to a more personal focus on understanding your strengths and vulnerabilities, self-care, and burn out.

Tools for Career Self-Evaluation

Career self-evaluation can take the form of reflection, journal writing, and unstructured conversations with others. In addition, structured tools may point you toward areas of self-discovery that you would not have considered otherwise. These include instruments described as *personality tests*, such as the California Personality Inventory (CPI). To take formal tests of this kind, you will need to meet with a psychologist or other qualified professional. Fortunately, there are also tools that you can learn about and use on your own, as well as the career-related tests described in Chapter 1.

Activities for Informal Exploration

The options described in this section can all be tried on your own, or with a counselor or other person who is familiar with them. All of them focus on you in your interpersonal context, which is a very important focus for human services professionals.

Hays's ADDRESSING Framework

Pamela Hays's ADDRESSING Framework (2016) is a great place to begin your self-exploration. Designed to help therapists consider the complexity of intersecting identities, it can also be used by interventionists to increase their understanding of their own intersecting and diverging groups. This model is helpful because it moves beyond common diversity characteristics, such as gender and ethnicity, by including areas that may not be visible or that we may forget are important, such as disability or national origin.

The acronym to help you remember the different areas to ask a client or yourself about is ADDRESSING (see Figure 2.1).

This model does not include some other aspects of diversity identity that many people find important, such as educational

---

Age and generational influences
Developmental disabilities
Disabilities (other)
Religion and spirituality
Ethnic and racial identity
Socioeconomic status
Sexual orientation
Indigenous heritage
National origin
Gender

FIGURE 2.1 The ADDRESSING Framework.

attainment. It is a good starting point, but be sure to add other factors and cultures that are important parts of your identity as well.

After you have described yourself using the ADDRESSING Framework, you may want to ask yourself questions such as the following:

- What parts of my identity stimulate me to want a career in human services? For example, you may respond, "As an African American female with a hidden disability, I have experienced discrimination. I want to work in human services in order to provide more sensitive community intervention systems." Or you might think, "I am a light-skinned Euro-American male from a middle-class family. I've had a lot of advantages, and my spiritual beliefs encourage me to help other people."

- Which aspects of my identity do I tend not to think about, and how can I be sure to remember them? For example, you might say, "I don't think about being born in the United States, and I realize that this is a form of privilege. Some of my clients will be born in other countries, so I need to think about this difference and ask all my clients about their experiences in this area."

- What parts of my identity have been unvalued or seen as an obstacle to the kind of work I want to do? Knowing about these barriers, what can I do to be a strategic student and job applicant? For example, you might think, "I am gay and I hope to have a career in the military, first as a Marine and then helping veterans at a community college. I can talk with my school's recruiter to find pre- and postenlistment resources for gay recruits."

- What aspects of my identity might make me a better or worse fit for human services positions that interest me? If the fit is better, how can I highlight and build on this? If the fit is worse, what can I do to address this? For example, you might respond, "I speak Spanish, which is a great job skill in the city where I want to work with immigrant families. I also know that there is a large Cambodian immigrant population there. How can I learn more about Cambodian culture?"

Just as importantly, you can use your ADDRESSING Framework to highlight aspects of your own identity that harmonize with each other and support your career goals, and those parts of yourself that may be in conflict with each other and create potential barriers to working toward those goals. For example, you may wonder, "I am a college-educated, majority-culture person. I am also Deaf. I want to be a mental health case manager for the county, but I worry that this isn't feasible. Whom can I contact to learn more about the kind of job I'm interested in and whether I can perform it with reasonable accommodations?" Or you might notice, "I meet all of the qualifications for a managerial job I want, but there's a part of me that says, 'If you're a woman in power, nobody will want to marry you.' I'd better talk to my counselor about this, because I want that job *and* I want a husband!"

Kliman's Social Matrix

If you would enjoy a more in-depth exploration of your own diverse identities, you can use Kliman's Social Matrix (2010). This tool uses a diagram to map a variety of identities and experiences, such as your family's income when you were a child and substance abuse issues, as well as your ADDRESSING (Hays, 2016) characteristics. In addition to bringing more identity factors and their influence to your attention, it also highlights your areas of relative privilege and marginalization. This can be a very useful starting point for the questions listed above as well. For the worksheet, instructions, and discussion of its uses, see Kliman's 2010 article.

The Genogram

A genogram (McGoldrick, Gerson, and Shellenberger, 1999) is a kind of annotated family tree. A standard family tree focuses on marriages and offspring. Its purpose is to show bloodlines and qualifications for inheritance, or to show family members' positions in the larger family. Family trees typically include names, dates of birth and death, marriages and partnerships, divorces and separations, and biological or adopted children.

The genogram's purposes are to include more information about the family of the index person (the person who is the focus of the exploration), and to characterize the significant relationships between these people. Genograms may include non-family members who are important to the index person, such as friends, counselors, and unrelated people living in the same household. Some people include their pets! In addition, genograms typically include standardized symbolic lines between people that show whether each relationship is close, distant, cut off, overly close, or conflictual, or has other important qualities. A genogram may include additional information, such as education, veteran status, physical and mental health, and any of the data captured by other tools such as Hays's ADDRESSING Framework (2016) or Kliman's Social Matrix (2010). They are frequently used by counselors, therapists, and social workers to stimulate conversation about their clients' relationships.

Constructing your own genogram can be very helpful for discovering cross-generational patterns (McGoldrick, Gerson, and Shellenberger, 1999), including educational and work patterns. For example, you might discover that in your extended family, girls and boys stop school at different ages, or that in every generation, one child follows a different career path from the other siblings. You may also discover that medical or psychological issues have influenced people's choices about moving, parenthood, or other factors that may affect career options. You may find that constructing your genogram reminds you that your cousin's spouse has a job that interests you, or that someone who is giving you negative feedback about your career has many conflictual relationships and may not be the most accurate source of information about your prospects.

You can learn more about genograms and how to construct them from *A Family Genogram Workbook* (Galindo, Boomer, and Reagan, 2006). Many electronic genogram-writing programs are available for purchase online as well. Genopro's website, https://www.

genopro.com/genogram/ (n.d.) includes an introduction to genograms and examples, in addition to reasonably priced genogram software.

The Johari Window

The Johari Window (Luft and Ingham, 1955) is often used in organizations to explore the relationship between our self-knowledge and the knowledge others have of us. While the original version is somewhat more structured and extensive, the Johari Window can also be used in an adapted form as a self-evaluation tool. This modification can still serve as a stimulus for conversations with friends, colleagues, or supervisors.

The modified version keeps the original's two-by-two square structure. One axis represents information about yourself that you know or don't know, and the other axis captures information that other people know or don't know about you. Filling in each quadrant helps illuminate areas where you may want to reveal or limit information about yourself (see Figure 2.2).

The adapted Johari Window diagram updates terms for some quadrants to bring them up to date. For example, the original version called the information unknown to oneself but known to others the "blind" quadrant, which is an outdated metaphor that is now offensive. Instead, some contemporary writers use "bad breath" to capture the idea of something others may know about you that you don't know about yourself. However, this image still implies that something may be wrong with you. Our adapted version uses "food on my face" to capture the potential embarrassment of other people seeing something about you that you don't know about, but without the suggestion that it is a serious problem. Some of the other quadrants are also renamed in more neutral or inclusive language.

To use this form of the Johari Window, start by thinking about how you present yourself in the classroom, at your internship, or at your job. Write a list of adjectives or descriptive phrases that express how you describe yourself and how other people have described you in this setting. For example, you might describe yourself as "honest," and you might know that your last evaluation said you were "hard working." When you've developed your list, put each term in the quadrant where you think it fits best. For example, if you wrote "worried about making mistakes" but you haven't told your supervisor about this, the information may fit in the "private" quadrant. Add items to your list and review their placement in the diagram over several days.

	Known to Self	Unknown to Self
Known to Others	OPEN	"FOOD ON MY FACE"
Unknown to Others	PRIVATE	NOT YET EXPLORED

FIGURE 2.2   Adapted Johari Window.

When you don't have more descriptions to add, you can use your completed diagram in several ways. First, you can consider whether you have a balance of positive and critical terms, or have included more of one than the other. If so, you may want to observe yourself in order to create a more balanced picture. Second, you can look at which quadrants include more items. While some quadrants are going to include guesses at this point, it is worth thinking about how you perceive other people's knowledge of you. Third, think about whether you want to change how many items are in each quadrant. Traditionally, this has meant asking yourself if you can decrease the number of "private" statements. However, you may also find that you have made some self-disclosures that you would like not to be so open about in the future, or that there are some aspects of yourself that you are happy to have kept from others. You will need to decide where your own comfort and boundaries are and when it is appropriate disclose or withhold information about yourself in a professional setting. Finally, you may want to share some or all of your diagram with someone you trust as a way to cross-check your fantasy about how other people see you and what they know about you.

The "not yet explored" quadrant, where neither you nor others know something about you, can be hard to fill out. Maybe you have not yet had the opportunity to explore and demonstrate an aspect of your professional self, or perhaps some aspect of yourself is not in the forefront of your consciousness and is not being demonstrated to other people. It may be helpful to speculate about what you and others might know about in the future.

Bronfenbrenner's Ecological Model

Urie Bronfenbrenner (1989) developed his *ecological model* as a way to describe how social and societal contexts influence a child's development. It is called "ecological" because it describes the person in his or her contexts, or "levels of the ecology." An adaptation of this model (Chronister, McWhirter, and Kerewsky, 2004) can be used as another form of self-assessment.

To start, focus on an aspect of your academic or professional life where you would like to understand your vulnerabilities and the lack of systemic support, as well as areas where you have good supports and strengths. For example, you might want to focus on "My Risk and Resilience in My New Practicum." Create two columns with six rows. Head the first column "Risk" and the second "Resilience."

+ First, consider your physical self—your body, gender, skin color, physical abilities and limitations, health, genetics, and temperament. Determine which of your physical characteristics may be a strength or area of vulnerability in relation to your area of focus. In the first row, list your physical risk factors or areas of vulnerability in the "Risk" column and your physical strengths and supported factors in the "Resilience" column. For example, you might put "I get strep a lot" in the first column and "I have excellent eyesight" in the second.

+ Second, make a list of the groups that are relevant to your area of focus. In this example, these might include other students in your class, your family, the other students at your practicum, and your practicum supervision group. List the major areas of vulnerability or difficulty, then strength or support, that each group provides to you. For example, "My children are unhappy that I am away from home so much" and "My supervisor and I have a good relationship." Try to list several examples in each column.

- + Third, think about how these groups interact (or don't interact) with each other. List areas of risk and resilience that arise from these interactions. For example, "My ex-wife called my professor and told her about our divorce" and "My academic advisor and my practicum program manager communicate throughout the term." Again, try to list several examples.
- + Fourth, think about the more impersonal systems that affect you but which you can't affect back directly. These include areas like the media, access to services, and laws. Generate your ideas. For example, "Professionals like the people at my practicum are depicted in many movies as unethical and unconcerned about clients" and "I received a scholarship that covers my tuition."
- + Fifth, think about your religious beliefs, ideas from your culture(s), societal values, and beliefs that just seem like common sense, such as "kindness is the greatest virtue" or "all people are equal." Which of these beliefs might affect you in this situation? You don't need to hold these beliefs—just be affected by them. For example, "Education is wasted on girls" and "My religion supports helping people to help themselves."
- + Finally, you may be experiencing or anticipating positive or negative change at one or more of these levels. List some areas of risk and resilience related to these changes. For example, "My practicum agency just lost funding, which jeopardizes my project" and "I passed my biology class and now have more time to go to staff trainings."

You have now identified some of your risk and resilience factors at each level of your ecology. Spend some time identifying additional strength and support factors at each level, then consider whether you can use any of these areas of resilience to help with your areas of risk or vulnerability. For example, could you talk with someone in your financial aid office to learn if you are eligible for more scholarships or financial support so that you could decrease your work hours and spend more time with your children? Sometimes it can be useful to shift your focus from what is going wrong to what is going right, opening new perspectives and possibilities for change. You may recognize this approach, where you ask what is already going well and whether you can get more of it, as a solution-focused intervention (e.g., Winbolt, 2003).

You can find a more technical description of the ecological model, with an example, in Chronister, McWhirter, and Kerewsky (2004), as well as illustrations of the model online.

The tools you've just explored derive from the general human services areas of counseling and management. They are great starting points for learning more about yourself and seeing how your personal and interpersonal characteristics may shape your career goals. Next, we will look at some more specific career and aptitude instruments that may be helpful for your targeted career exploration.

Evaluating Your Career Strengths and Areas of Competence, Part 2

As you have already learned, career counselors can help you learn about your job skills and preferences, identify related jobs with which you may not be familiar, and provide resources for your job search. If your school doesn't have a career center, remember that you may be able to use career counseling resources at your local community college, university, or governmental employment office.

Career Counseling for Self-Exploration

In addition to the career-specific tests described in Chapter 1, career counselors can administer additional tests and instruments. This section describes three widely used career counseling instruments that are a good fit with your earlier self-exploration: the Myers-Briggs Type Indicator® (Myers & Myers, 1995), the FIRO-B® (Career Assessment Site, 2017), and the Big Five Personality Test (cf. Howard and Howard, 2000). These are *normative* instruments, meaning that unlike many tests used in clinical psychology, they describe a range of normal characteristics, rather than serving as a way to differentiate between normal and abnormal personality traits or behaviors. As compared to the career exploration-specific tools in Chapter 1, these are used for broader purposes than just career counseling, although they often are part of a career testing battery as well.

Unlike the tools presented earlier in this chapter, these instruments have been studied extensively and use comparisons of your responses with those of other people as part of the underlying test structure that generates your results.

Myers-Briggs Type Indicator® (MBTI®)

The Myers-Briggs Type Indicator® (MBTI®) asks questions that sort out your preferences in order to construct one of 16 types. They are called *personality types*, but they are actually *preference types*. Each type is represented by a 4-letter code. For example, an ENFJ code means that the person's preferences for interacting, using information, decision-making, and degree of structure can be described as Extraverted, Intuitive, Feeling, and Judging. An ISTP code refers to a person whose preferences can be described as Introverted, Sensing, Thinking, and Perceiving. There are 14 other possible type combinations of these codes. None of the types is good or bad. They are all descriptive and based on your answers.

Your code type is a shorthand way to explain how you prefer to interact with the world, other people, and tasks. Some jobs are easier or more enjoyable when their requirements, and organizational culture, are close to your MTBI® type. If your type is, generally speaking, a good match for your job, you are more likely to experience satisfaction, know what is expected of you, and be successful. If your job is not a good fit for your type, you may still find it enjoyable and be successful in it, but this might require more compromise and energy, and your work may not be as satisfying or meaningful to you.

For example, a person who leads skill-building groups for teens with attention deficits may find the job easier if she is extraverted and likes to focus on other people. A commonly used metaphor for this aspect of extraversion is that the person needs to get her batteries charged by interacting with people. An introverted person could do this job,

Preferences, Not Limitations

Dr. Schwartz is the professor in charge of training the graduate psychology students who will provide the on-campus supervision groups for his incoming undergraduate human services students. Although Dr. Schwartz has not yet met either group of students, he knows from his previous experience in these two academic programs that the majority of his human services students will have a MBTI® type that is extraverted, intuitive, feeling, and judging (ENFJ), but the majority of the graduate psychology students will be introverted, that those in the research track may be more sensing and thinking in their preferences, and that the ones who hope to become psychotherapists will tend toward perceiving.

Dr. Schwartz knows that these are trends, not individual types, and that these trends represent potential preferences, not abilities. He himself is a psychologist with a research focus, but he is extraverted and loves working with groups. His research program involves forms of participatory action research, which includes talking with community members and utilizes his extraverted preference. When it is time to analyze his data, he is able to sit down and do so, although he makes sure he schedules meetings with his co-investigators and research assistants to talk about the analysis because he enjoys this and it keeps him on track. Dr. Schwartz knows from his own professional experience that a MBTI® type is a preference, not a limitation on a person's skills and abilities.

When he meets with the graduate students who will be supervising the undergraduates, he asks them to take the MBTI® using the college's online career resources. Dr. Schwartz, who is trained to interpret career tests, then has the students review their obtained types to see if they seem to describe each person accurately. He has them group themselves in different ways according to parts of their types and have conversations about their problem-solving strategies, forms of creativity, ways they track assignments and time management strategies, desire for interpersonal interactions, quickness to form hypotheses, and other preferences reflected by their MBTI® types. Not surprisingly, most of the graduate students are either introverted or only slightly extraverted. They vary on other characteristics, but most of them report that they are quiet, like to listen, and prefer to think things through before acting or making a decision.

Dr. Schwartz turns the discussion to the graduate students' supervisory job responsibilities. He lets them know that their undergraduates are likely to be ENFJs. He challenges them to talk with a partner and develop strategies for bridging the type differences so that the undergraduate students' needs will be met in a way that fits their preferences and the

(continued)

graduate students will not feel exhausted or frustrated. After pair discussions, the group reconvenes and shares their ideas. These include the following:

- Ask (but don't require) the undergraduates to take the MBTI®.
- Have a career counselor, trained faculty member, or advanced graduate student visit the supervision groups to present on the basics of MBTI® type and have students informally evaluate their potential type in order to foster a discussion.
- Self-disclose their types to their students and have a conversation about how to meet the needs of all students in that supervision group.
- Do not self-disclose type, but lead a similar discussion, perhaps using exercises supplied by the career center.
- Do not have a discussion, but be aware of student preferences and lead activities to help them identify those preferences and strengths, possible problems related to over-relying on some strengths, and identifying and developing their use of less-preferred skills and areas of focus.

Dr. Schwartz also reminds the graduate students that they will be structuring and presenting part of the undergraduate orientation training, and that this will be the first time the undergraduates meet them. He asks what their ideas are for joining their students, thinking from an MBTI® perspective. Many good ideas are generated, including emails later in the week from the graduate students who wanted to think about it on their own. The graduate students present a list of ideas to Dr. Schwartz and let him know that they have all agreed that they can "channel our inner ENFJ camp counselor" during the introductory activity.

When the human services students evaluate their orientation, several comment on the "energetic, bubbly" supervisors, who "really connected" with them "even though some of them said they're normally pretty quiet." Others say that they "appreciate that the supervisors said that all of us are different and that we'll work together in supervision group to make sure it works for everybody. That's great because I can already tell that I like to listen and a lot of my classmates like to talk!"

but he might feel more drained and lose more energy by the end of the day. It's not that he can't do it, but that he prefers smaller groups, one-to-one interventions, or to work with a different client population. Or maybe he just needs some down time after group to quietly write his notes. Similarly, someone may be a fantastic and dynamic teacher, but have a hard time following the required curriculum because he is intuitive rather than sensing and often has ideas that are more innovative and interesting than the ones he is supposed to teach. This doesn't mean that he can't follow the requirements, but he may need the insight that this is not always his preference, and maybe some help, such as checking in with a supervisor at the end of the week to review what he did in class and adjust the upcoming lessons. Of course, he might also decide that he wants to teach or lead workshops in an environment where he has more opportunities to deviate from his outline. Your MBTI® type is not a deal breaker! Rather, it helps you identify and articulate areas of relative goodness of fit between your preferred style and the demands of a task or job responsibility.

As you may have guessed already, the MBTI® is often used in counseling to help clients gain insight into their relationships and to explore why they sometimes experience conflicts. This is important information in your personal relationships and also extremely useful for understanding more about how you interact with other people at work. For this reason, the MBTI® is a popular tool for use in staff trainings and workplace interventions intended to improve employees' relationships and provide nonjudgmental descriptions of conflicts, as well as to point toward ways to resolve them. It is easy to learn and understand MBTI® basics.

Side Box 2.2

An MBTI® Resource

You may enjoy the book *Gifts Differing: Understanding Personality Type* (Myers and Myers, 1995) for a very readable overview of the MBTI®. For a more professional perspective, including current resources, try The Myers and Briggs Foundation website at http://www.myersbriggs.org/.

FIRO-B®

Although it is not used as frequently as the other tests in this section, FIRO-B® (CAS, 2017) may be useful if you are experiencing interpersonal conflicts at work, your field site placement, or at school, since it is often used to explore workplace groups and preferences. This test characterizes your comfort and desires related to interpersonal inclusion, control, and affection, both as you prefer them and as you express them. You can see a sample report at the CAS website.

FIRO-B® is sometimes paired with the MBTI® to help managers, supervisors, and work or other groups to understand how each person's preferred interpersonal style and decision-making may interact with others' styles. Understanding these interactions tends to neutralize conflicts between group members (or members and supervisors), which decreases conflict and helps the group use its members' strengths. It can help group or work team leaders to learn about their interpersonal preferences in order to become more effective in their leadership role.

Big Five Personality Test

The Big Five Personality Test (Truity, 2017) is based on a small number of personality traits derived from a large sample of responses to questions. It works well cross-culturally and, like the MBTI®, may be useful for understanding how you interact with people at work and the types of work that may be a good fit for your results. The Big Five tells you how much of each of its five factors you have reported—Openness, Conscientiousness, Extraversion, Agreeableness, and Neuroticism (the Neuroticism scale is sometimes presented reversed because it is a negative trait, so you may also see it labeled "Non-neuroticism"). An easy way to remember the factors is with the acronym OCEAN.

As in the MBTI®, there are no wrong or right answers, but a person who is low on Agreeableness or high on Neuroticism (low on Non-neuroticism) may have a hard time in some human services positions. This does not mean that no human services job would be a good fit, but finding a match might be more challenging. For example, someone with a low Agreeableness score might have interpersonal conflicts and not be successful as a case worker, but might do well as a quality assurance reviewer, grant writer, or in other behind-the-scenes roles. It is also important to consider that someone with high Agreeableness may be too trusting or yielding to be a good unit manager, for example.

Multiple sites offer free versions of the Big Five (for example, Truity, 2017, at https://www.truity.com/test/big-five-personality-test and OutOfService (n.d.) at https://www.outofservice.com/bigfive/). Don't forget that the term *neuroticism* as used in the Big Five is not a diagnosis and does not mean that a high scorer meets the criteria for any neurotic disorder.

Free Online Career and Preference Tests

While there is normally a cost associated with the MBTI®, the Big Five and similar instruments can be found online for free, sometimes associated with research studies. If you are going to try the Big Five or a Big Five-like test on your own, be sure to read the informed consent document, and be aware that sometimes the language used can sound pejorative or feel humiliating. For this reason, it is best to talk with someone you trust about your results if you choose to take this test on your own.

Other Career and Vocational Assessments

Many other instruments for exploring your career preferences, aptitudes, and personality-job match are available at career centers, as described in Chapter 1.

Your career strengths and areas of competence are likely to map onto your MBTI® type and Big Five profile reasonably well. If you are at the beginning of your human services career and still not certain which strengths you have, these and other career instruments can help you identify jobs that are a good match for your results, and therefore more likely to be a good fit that builds on your preferences and areas of competence. If you are shifting to human services from a different field, they should help you identify your transferable skills and learn how your preferences are used in your new profession. Finally, if you are a long-time human services professional looking for your next step, they should help you explore your less-utilized areas of competence, stretch yourself, and identify meaningful directions for your job search.

Understanding Your Triggers and Vulnerabilities

As noted earlier, many people enter the human services field because their own experiences inspire them to help others. This sense of mission and desire to give back or correct systemic problems is laudable and ethical. Whether or not your personal experiences motivate you toward a human services career, everyone has areas of alarm, vulnerability, and lack of insight. In addition to the tools described above, you have many sources of information about areas where you need to expand your knowledge and skills. These include your grades and feedback from your instructors, supervisors, and clients, as well as your honest self-reflection.

While everyone has risk in some areas and resilience in others, some people have a harder time maintaining their emotional balance. You may have always been more easily upset, or had a harder time processing information or emotions (this is an example of a risk factor at the first level of the ecological model). You may have had family difficulties as a child, such as separation from your parent, substance abuse in your home, or interpersonal violence (risks at the second level of your ecology). There are many other reasons why you may find yourself triggered by aspects of human services work. Acknowledging your vulnerabilities is a good first step toward resolving them so that you can function well and do work that you find meaningful.

Transference, Countertransference, and Ethical Practice

Transference and *countertransference* are terms that originally come from the field of psychoanalysis. For our purposes, *transference* refers to feelings, thoughts, and beliefs that a client (or student or supervisee) has about the interventionist (or teacher or supervisor) that reflect a previous relationship of the client's more strongly than the actual relationship the client has with the interventionist. Similarly, *countertransference* refers to a phenomenon in which the interventionist responds to a client as if the client is someone from the interventionist's life. In both cases, the important factor is that the person is interacting with the other person symbolically rather than realistically. Sometimes this takes the form of thoughts such as "He's just like my wonderful [or horrible] father!" Another common form is when a client believes that the interventionist is more like herself than he actually is, or when the interventionist makes the same mistake. In this situation, your underlying thought process might be something like "I am Baptist and my instructor is Baptist, so we share all the same values and are similar in many other ways."

Unexpectedly Triggered

Julia worked hard to overcome her very difficult childhood. Her father, who had bipolar disorder, sometimes became paranoid. He would drive to her school, certain that she was in danger, and burst into her classroom to rescue her. When she was little, he would drag her to the car and drive out of state, where they would hide in state parks until he became depressed. Then, Julia would steal his phone and call her stepmother. As Julia grew up, her father's manic episodes became more agitated and angry. When she resisted his "rescues," he would sometimes hit her. Eventually, child protective services stepped in. Julia's father and stepmother divorced, and she moved with her stepmother to another state during one of her father's psychiatric hospitalizations.

Although she grew up to have a passion for helping children, Julia knew that it would be too difficult for her to work with traumatized youth or parents with mental illnesses. She talked with her academic advisor, and they were able to identify sites that had a more normative focus for her required child/adolescent and adult field site placements. Her child/adolescent placement in an after-school arts program for students from low-income families went well, and Julia hoped to return as an employee after she graduated.

About three weeks into Julia's adult placement at a food bank, an unexpected event occurred. A woman burst into the warehouse where Julia was checking food pallets against lists for distribution sites. The woman screamed that the apocalypse had come and that everyone must repent. Although her coworkers quickly and effectively ushered the woman out of the warehouse and talked with her until a crisis counselor arrived from a nearby agency, Julia was paralyzed. She had not had an anxiety attack in many years, but she was overwhelmed by panic. When she could move, she fled from the warehouse. She couldn't focus enough to find her car, so she ran to the bus station and got on the next bus pulling out, although she didn't know where she was going.

When Julia's head cleared, she realized she was in a strange town without any money or identification. She spotted a medical clinic, explained that she had lost her wallet, and asked to use the phone to call her roommate. Her roommate picked her up, but Julia refused to return to the warehouse and crawled into bed. She was angry at her father, at herself, and at the woman, even though she also recognized that the woman was distressed and needed help.

Knowing in her heart that she had destroyed her chances for a human services career and would probably fail her practicum class as well, Julia

(continued)

refused to get out of bed, answer her phone, or eat for two days. She ruminated about how her life was destroyed and had bad dreams about her father. Her worried roommate called Julia's stepmother, who let herself into the apartment, talked Julia into the shower, and made her a sandwich. After Julia poured out her story, her stepmother encouraged her to call her field site supervisor.

Julia's supervisor was relieved to hear from her. She told Julia that her purse was safe in her office, and expressed empathic concern for Julia's well-being. She let Julia know that she had spoken to Julia's campus supervisor and encouraged Julia to let him know that she was okay. She offered to meet Julia and give her back her purse in the parking lot of a fast food restaurant near the warehouse, "because I'll bet you don't want to go back in there right now!" Julia and her stepmother went to the restaurant, where the supervisor normalized Julia's fear and provided some counseling resources. She told Julia that she could reassign her to a different location.

Encouraged by this, Julia emailed her campus supervisor, who was also relieved to hear from her and gave her some websites for managing panic. When she returned to campus the next day, he helped her write emails to the instructors whose classes she had missed. He also told her, "I'm sorry that happened to you because I know why we chose these sites for you. Today isn't the time for it, but I'd like to help you find ways to manage triggers you can't anticipate. Stuff happens, and I want to be sure you have as many coping skills as possible!"

Julia's supervisors' resources and reassurances were supportive. Julia was highly motivated to use those resources to decrease the intensity of her response in unexpected situations when adults' heightened emotional reactions triggered visceral memories of her childhood.

Transference and countertransference are problematic for human services workers because they are perceptions that are based in positive or negative fantasies. In a long-term therapy relationship, exploring this can be valuable. However, human services workers often have limited time to work with their clients, and in their job roles, it is often inappropriate to engage in deep psychological conversations. Alert professionals notice when a client may be seeing them as if they are someone else, and take steps to draw attention to the current and real relationship. Even more importantly, human services professionals need to monitor themselves to be certain that they are really seeing each client and not projecting feelings, thoughts, and beliefs onto them that are actually about other people. This includes positive countertransference as well. If you forget that your client is your client, and who he is as a person, because when you are with him you feel like you did when you were a child with your brother, you may forget your role responsibilities and fail to hold him accountable, for example.

Human services professionals have ethical responsibilities related to competence (National Organization for Human Services, 2015). If you do not really see your clients, you are not practicing competently.

Self-Care and Avoiding Burnout

Another important ethical responsibility is self-care. As Standard 35 of the Ethical Standards for Human Services Professionals states, "Human service professionals strive to develop and maintain healthy personal growth to ensure that they are capable of giving optimal services to clients" (National Organization for Human Services, 2015; see also Appendix B). This standard can be hard to follow at times, but it is very important to keep it in mind. Your self-care and self-exploration increase your own equilibrium, energy for your work, and ability to see clients for who they really are so that you can help address their needs.

Some people slide into problematic and unhelpful strategies under the guise of self-care. These can include procrastinating or failing to complete work such as documenting client encounters or submitting billing sheets, drinking or using other substances in an attempt to manage or avoid emotions, or failing to do parts of their job. All of these inappropriate responses to stress jeopardize their clients, their agency's reputation, and themselves.

In addition to your emotional and interpersonal self-care, you need to attend to your physical well-being. This means paying attention to activities that affect your health, including what you eat, your sleep hygiene, not abusing substances (including coffee!), exercising, meditating, engaging in physical stress reduction activities, and similar actions. Many human services trainees and professionals find it helpful to see a therapist, engage in group counseling, or participate in a peer consultation group for support, feedback, and an environment in which they can be frank about their vulnerabilities.

The Adverse Childhood Experiences Study (ACES) demonstrated that "childhood experiences, both positive and negative, have a tremendous impact on future violence victimization and perpetration, and lifelong health and opportunity" (Centers for Disease Control, April 1, 2016). This is as true for you as it is for your clients. Learning about ACES from reputable sources such as the Substance Abuse and Mental Health Services Administration (SAMHSA, September 5, 2017) may help you to focus your own self-help activities. You can take the ACE questionnaire online at https://acestoohigh.com/got-your-ace-score/ (Aces Too High, n.d.). Similarly, learning about interventions that are helpful for at-risk youth (e.g., McWhirter, McWhirter, McWhirter, & McWhirter, 2017) may give you some tools to use for yourself so that you can be more resilient and available to help your clients.

Sometimes, human services students or young professionals complain that they are suffering from burnout. Often what they mean is that their self-care has temporarily not kept up with their job requirements and work stressors, or that their work stress currently exceeds their self-care resources, or that they no longer like their jobs.

However, some of the time they are indeed experiencing true burnout, which can be defined as more enduring "emotional exhaustion, depersonalization, and diminished sense of personal efficacy" (Tuma, 2017). It may be helpful to think about burnout as losing your positive emotions about your work, as well as becoming negative, cynical, depressed, or angry about it.

Burnout is distressing for you and can erode the quality of care you give your clients. For example, a recent study of about 6,700 medical doctors reported that the doctors with even one symptom of burnout had made twice as many medical errors in the previous three months (Haelle, July 9, 2018). Noticing that you are moving toward burnout and then applying your self-help skills may often be sufficient to reverse the trend. Looking for ways to head off burnout, such as talking to your supervisor, changing job responsibilities, or taking a vacation, may also help.

A program called Three Good Things seems to help some people reverse burnout. "[R]esearchers ask each [health care worker] volunteer to write down, just before going to bed, three good things that happened that day and label them with one of the 10 positive emotions that have been most closely tied to burnout: joy, gratitude, serenity, interest, hope, pride, amusement, inspiration, awe, and love" (Tuma, 2017). This intervention decreased burnout for some people in less than two weeks.

Another suggestion for reversing burnout is to reflect and be mindful, have supportive work relationships, and decrease your isolation (Melton, 2017). The good news is that the self-care activities described above, such as taking care of yourself physically, may also reduce burnout.

Side Box 2.4

Learn About and Manage Your Negative Emotions and Experiences

- If you would like to learn more about the physiological bases of stress, insomnia, pain, depression, and related topics, read Robert M. Sapolsky's *Why Zebras Don't Get Ulcers* (2004).

- Jon Kabat-Zinn's *Full Catastrophe Living: Using the Wisdom of Your Body and Mind to Face Stress, Pain, and Illness* (2013) is a wonderful research-based sourcebook on mindfulness activities to improve health and reduce stress.

- Michael Carroll's *Awake at Work: 35 Practical Buddhist Principles for Discovering Clarity and Balance in the Midst of Work's Chaos* (2006) describes how you can become more engaged with your work and less vulnerable to the inevitable frustrations and challenges of any workplace.

Using Self-Help, Counseling, and Other Interventions

Thousands of self-help books and workbooks are available from bookstores and online. This is a great resource for your clients—and for you, too. You may want to read at least a few self-help books that help you address your own issues. In addition to helping yourself, your deeper understanding of these resources will allow you to make better recommendations to your clients.

This sort of "experience from the inside" also applies to counseling. Entering counseling might be a good source of support for you, and it may give you a better sense of when to suggest counseling to your clients. If relevant to your own issues, you may want to attend a peer-led or leaderless group, such as a 12-step meeting.

Writing, art, and other creative pursuits may also be ways to explore yourself, find balance in your life, and refresh yourself in the face of work stress. No matter what combination of activities you choose for self-exploration and support, you will have the satisfaction of knowing that by putting this time and effort into yourself, you are also becoming a more skillful, self-aware, and ethical professional.

Questions for Career Self-Reflection

This chapter has included many questions and tools for career exploration. Here are more questions to further this process:

+ What appeals to me about human services work in general?
+ Am I drawn to particular issues? Why?
+ Am I drawn to particular populations? Why?
+ Do I want a career in human services, or is this something that other people think I should do? Is it something I think I should want to do?
+ How do I balance my career goals with other people's ideas about my career? Whose preferences are important for me to consider?
+ What are my areas of competence and resilience? How can I build on them and use them to address my areas of risk and vulnerability?
+ Do I have triggers that will make some human services roles difficult for me? What do I need to do now to reduce the effects of those triggers so that I can be a competent professional?
+ When have I noticed transference and countertransference in my own academic and work life? In what areas, or with what kinds of people, will I need to monitor myself to be sure I am seeing the real person?
+ Do I sometimes find it difficult to let my clients choose solutions and approaches that are different from my preferences?
+ Am I ready to practice in this field? How will I know when I am psychologically and emotionally able to focus on my client's needs rather than becoming overwhelmed or absorbed in my own?

- Are there ways to limit my exposure to triggering situations while I work on normalizing my reactions? Do I need to take some time off from my program or discuss a term without a placement with my advisor?
- How have I used self-help, counseling, and other interventions in the past? What specific forms of self-care would be helpful for me now?

Figure Credits

Fig. 2.1: Pamela A. Hays, Addressing Cultural Complexities in Practice: Assessment, Diagnosis, and Therapy. Copyright © 2016 by American Psychological Association.

Fig. 2.2: Adapted from Joseph Luft and H. Ingham, The Johari Window: A Graphic Model of Interpersonal Awareness. Copyright © 1955 by Los Angeles: UCLA Extension Office.

Chapter 3

Be Strategic

Why Strategize?

Although the world of professional work can seem far away when you're a student, graduation is coming up faster than you might anticipate. It's important to think ahead so that you can identify and use your resources, keep track of requirements, and choose training sites and experiences that will contribute to your career development. Even as a student, you can begin to connect with your professional communities. You may not know exactly what type of human services job you want after graduation, but having a flexible plan will help you stay on track and decrease the possibility of disappointing surprises.

Utilize Your Program and Institutional Resources

Your academic program and school provide a number of very useful opportunities for learning more about careers in human services, as well as exploring your own preferences. Be sure to take advantage of these resources, many or all of which are free for enrolled students.

Your Program Handbook

Most human services programs have a handbook for admitted students. Reading the handbook is an effective way to get an overview of the program. This will help you plan your time in the program in order to explore and work toward your career goals. If your program does not have a student handbook, ask where you will find information about program requirements, field site placements, competencies, grievance procedures, how to remain in good standing, and other governance documents. Your program may publish this information on a website, or provide handouts at orientation or in classes.

The handbook may vary across entering cohorts, so be sure that you use the version intended for the date you entered your program. You may be able to read a current handbook online or request a copy from an academic advisor or a student services coordinator. Comparing several handbooks, as well as using the other resources in this section, may guide your decision about which program(s) to apply to. Remember that the program's curriculum, requirements, and other features are likely to change over time. The program is only bound to the standards of the handbook for the cohort in which you are admitted. Many excellent programs do not include some of the topics below in their handbooks. You may want to make a list of questions as you read so that you can follow up with an academic advisor or other representative.

Program Accreditation

Your handbook is likely to include information about whether your program is accredited by an organization that provides oversight and quality control, such as the Council for Standards in Human Service Education (CSHSE, 2010). It may also inform you of national licenses or certifications for which successful completion of the program will qualify you, such as the Human Services–Board Certified Practitioner (HS–BCP) certificate offered by the Center for Credentialing & Education (CCE, 2016b). Your program may also meet educational requirements that will allow you to apply for state-issued licenses or certificates, or for the state's job-linked professional designations such as the Qualified Mental Health Associate (QMHA) status. (QMHA requirements vary. Check your state's requirements online.) Job characteristics, license or certificate, and designation requirements may change over time or differ across states. If you're not sure whether the handbook is up to date or if the program will meet the requirements of a different state, talk with program personnel. Your handbook may also include a list of faculty and staff members' contact information and their roles in the program. This information will help you find the right people to answer your questions.

CSHSE accreditation requirements set many of the standards for program faculty, courses and training experiences, retaining or dismissing students, and related program parameters (CSHSE, 2018). If your program is not accredited, you can review these standards to get a sense of the requirements for an accredited program or one that follows most or all of the standards even if it is not accredited.

"Informed Consent for Being a Student"

Most handbooks will present some material that could be called *informed consent for being a student*. This may include information such as background check requirements or other legal requirements and restrictions for admitted students, expectations for student behavior, ethical standards and legal issues such as mandated reporting, criteria to remain in good academic standing, criteria for removal from the program, grievance processes, equity and inclusion policies, how to request academic disability accommodation, and other program or institutional standards. Some of this information may appear elsewhere. For example, some course syllabi will include statements about the degree of self-disclosure that is required for that class. Because it is so important, you may want to ask where you will find any information of this type that is not in the handbook.

Some applicants have been convicted of misdemeanors or felonies. The handbook may provide information about background check requirements and which convictions may prevent you from being admitted to the program. Admitted students with convictions may not be permitted to engage in field placements at some sites, or may encounter obstacles to entering some graduate programs or obtaining certain licensed or certificates. If this important information is not available in the handbook, contact the person who is listed as a resource for applicants or new students, or someone in program leadership who can answer your questions.

Classes and Other Requirements

Handbooks typically provide a great deal of academic information. This may include required courses, electives and courses that may be substituted, a sample or required course sequence, program and institutional graduation requirements, advising handouts, grading information, and professional competencies met by your classes and training placements. They may also include information about study abroad opportunities or international training sites.

You may also find information about placement requirements and opportunities. These may be called *field site, placement, field study, practicum, internship, externship, cooperative education placement, service-learning* or other terms. These placements may begin immediately or later in your program. Some may have prerequisites, or a class or supervision seminar that must be taken along with the placement. Some may be reserved for beginning or advanced students, or meet requirements such as a lifespan training, work with a specific population, or training in a particular skill or competency. Some placements require a more extensive background check than your program's admissions requirement. Others may not permit you to complete a placement at a site where you also have a paid job or where you already volunteer. Application processes and requirements vary greatly across programs and sites, so you will want to know your program's policies and those of sites that interest you.

Special Graduation Requirements

If a program requires a capstone project, comprehensive exams, or an exit exam, this information should appear in the handbook as well. A capstone project is a wonderful product for demonstrating an area of particular focus or expertise, so if your program includes one, you can also plan ahead to identify possible projects that will support your career goals.

Policies Related to Good Standing and Problem Areas

In addition to a description of how a student remains in good standing in the program (or links to the school's student conduct code and relevant policies), your handbook should explain how enrolled students are evaluated for advancement and graduation. This should include the processes for a student who needs to file a grievance or complaint. It should also outline the steps the program will take to determine that there is a student-related problem, when remediation will be offered, how the remediation will be evaluated, and the circumstances under which a student may be asked to take a leave of absence or be removed from the program. The handbook should explain the steps in a way that is easy for an average student to understand. There should be no mysteries related to these processes.

Resources for Students

Finally, your handbook may provide other resources and referrals, both on and off campus. These may include academic offices such as the registrar, student support services such as the counseling center, student organizations such as a Black students' union or ballroom dance club, and other services such as legal assistance, a housing office, or sources of emergency food boxes or medical care.

"Informed Consent for Students" Is an Ongoing Process

If you are already admitted to your program, it is a good idea to review your handbook periodically as you progress through your program and different sections become more important. This should be a reminder to be alert to any changes in the program that may affect you. These changes may be posted on the program's website, emailed, or announced in a class or meeting. It's a good idea to collect documentation for any information that is a change from your handbook.

Academic Advisors

Academic advisors are another good source of information. If you are having trouble sorting out information from your handbook or online, they can help you narrow down your search and find what you need. They are experts at sorting through large amounts of sometimes contradictory information, and they are often aware of upcoming changes. They are skillful at helping you see the big picture and move toward your goals. Some programs have their own advisors, while others may have departmental or even school-wide advisors. The more closely they are affiliated with your academic program, the more likely they are to know all the ins and outs of your major.

Academic advisors can help you determine your schedule of required and elective courses to be sure you will meet your program and school requirements. They may have, or be able to direct you to, advising handouts or checklists. They may suggest classes or activities that will help you get a job or apply for graduate programs. They can answer questions about your program or institution's accreditation, any additional or alternative classes available, or where to find other academic information for your program or school requirements. They may be familiar with different classes and instructors, so they may be able to answer questions about course content, assignments, or teaching styles. Academic advisors may also have suggestions for how to track your completion of academic requirements.

You might have a very clear idea of what you want to do after you finish your degree, or you may still be exploring the field. Your academic advisor may be able to investigate more options or refer you to your career center for counseling and testing as described in Chapters 1 and 2.

Sometimes college students who are having a hard time emotionally also approach academic advisors, since career and personal goals and issues are often interrelated (Shallcross, 2013). Your advisor may refer you to a faculty member or on- or off-campus counselor, depending upon campus resources and your concerns. Since your emotional state and stressors may affect your academics, it is good to get referrals so that you can have the best college experience possible, and be ready for the challenges of graduation and your job search.

Program Website and Institutional Resources

Your program's website may provide additional, updated information. It may have links to faculty biographies and websites, policies, the handbook, advising handouts, forms, and local resources. If your program is part of a department or a college in a university, there may be links to related programs, including other classes and student groups that may interest to you. For example, you might discover that a program in the building next to yours offers sign language training that both meets your school's language requirement and is a prerequisite for applying to a practicum with Deaf children at an attached clinic.

Your program or department may bring in guest speakers or trainers whose presentations relate to your career goals. Don't miss these opportunities to learn from professionals, including people whom you may want to contact for advice or job shadowing, or because their agency is hiring. Presentations are also a good opportunity to see which other students are also interested in the topics that stimulate you.

College and university websites can be extensive and difficult to navigate. Ask an advisor, friend, or consultant from a relevant college office to help you get started or identify key words that will retrieve the results you need.

In addition to academic programs, colleges have offices you may recognize, such as counseling, career services, accessible education or disability services, financial aid, library services, and study abroad, for example. Deans, student housing, parking, the registrar, the president and provost, and other administrative offices may also have websites describing policies and services they provide. Student organizations typically have a web presence as well, whether they are group- and identity-based, such as a Black student union; activity-based such as a student hiking club; or service-based, such as a renters' rights office.

College websites may also provide forms and documents for admissions and enrolled students, job listings, scholarship information, faculty and student profiles, online student publications, and much more. It is worth spending some time exploring your college's website. As a bonus, you may locate offices and organizations that are a good fit for your career interests. If so, ask your advisor or placement coordinator if an on-campus placement can be arranged.

Remarks From a Current Student

A student recently shared her academic program experience:

> "One of the things I really appreciate about this program is the emphasis on professionalism and being a professional-in-training even while we're still students. I've learned a lot about how to present myself. When I needed to attend a meeting about an institutional concern I was raising, I made sure to dress professionally, I had all of the paperwork organized and with me, and I treated people respectfully even though I was frustrated.
>
> "The program has been so beneficial to me. I have already been able to implement the things I have learned in my current position, as well as at home with my husband and teenagers."

Peers

The best source of information about your program and career options may be your classmates. You might not think so when you look around the room during your first class meeting, but very soon you will all be each other's coworkers. You will make referrals to each other's agencies, supervise each other, and hire each other to provide professional development or consultation for your agency.

Your cohort is an effective place to network. You can also learn a great deal about types of jobs you had not known about or hadn't considered in your early career exploration. Your classmate may want to train at a site where you worked, or a group of students may identify an unmet need in the community and decide to start a new agency.

Your classes and other program meetings are an excellent place to make your transition from student to professional. There are many benefits to thinking of yourself as a professional-in-training during your program, and acting accordingly. Students may show up for class in their pajamas and with unbrushed teeth, or roll their eyes to express disagreement, or skip class because they were up too late the night before. None of these are professional behaviors, but like anything else, professionalism takes practice. You can use your years in your program to make your professional comportment more automatic. You may find that acting like a professional in the classroom makes it easier to talk with your instructors and site supervisors. When you show human services faculty that you are working actively toward your program's competencies, including professional self-presentation, you may get better reference letters. When you show your site supervisors and other staff that you understand that you are a professional-in-training, you may move yourself up on a hiring list. When your classmates see you as an ethical professional, they will want to network with you.

Present Yourself Professionally

The other perspective is also true. If you present yourself at school and with your class-mates as unprofessional, undisciplined, unethical, or difficult to work with, you will have a reputation for being unready to work in the field. Doing assignments at the last minute, letting down your peers on a group assignment, being unprepared for class, plagiarizing or other forms of academic dishonesty, active substance use problems, disrespectful interactions with others, inattention to diversity and equity, and other ethical and legal problems establish you as untrustworthy and as an undesirable colleague. Sometimes your peers are concerned about you and the welfare of your clients, and may bring their concerns to faculty. Since your program is responsible for your actions at your training site, lack of professionalism may also lead your faculty to slow down your program or remove you from the major. Although this is not common, it does happen. Maintaining your professionalism keeps more of your options open.

The behaviors expected of you as a professional-in-training will vary depending upon your program, and even the region of the country. If you are not sure how to conduct yourself at school or at your training site, ask your peers, faculty, and site supervisor.

A problematic aspect of relying only on your peers is that sometimes they give you incorrect information, leading to confusion and difficulties. If anything you hear sounds too good (or too bad) to be true, check it out with a faculty or staff member.

College is like a workplace in many ways. Use your time as a student to notice the structure of your program and school, the flow of information, who makes decisions, how well policies are implemented, how vulnerable people are supported, and other phenomena that help you assess a potential placement or job and increase your sophistication as a human services employee.

A Note to First-Generation College Students

If you are the first person in your family to attend college, you may be at a disadvantage compared to your peers. Parents (and even older siblings) who have been to college know something about college culture, including some of the expectations, timelines, resources, and pathways to success associated with specific academic programs or the larger institu-tion. Although their college experiences may differ from their children's, it is a starting point. First-generation students may not be aware of deadlines, prerequisites, or a variety of things a college assumes you already know. See if your school has a nontraditional student office that can answer questions that you may not even know to ask! If there is no office, use the resources in this chapter to orient yourself. Be sure your academic advisors know that you are a first-generation college student so that they can point you toward resources for understanding college culture and requirements.

Getting the Most From Your Site Placements

Another important arena for career exploration and preparation is your site placements, which will be called by different terms (for example, *field study, practicum, internship,*

Harry Potter, First-Generation Student

What do wizards do? Although first-generation student Hermione Granger probably knows, Harry Potter doesn't (Rowling, 1998). Although Harry's parents attended Hogwarts, he was orphaned long before they could pass on advice about school success and wizarding careers. Harry is years into his education before any institutional career advising occurs (Rowling, 2003). By then it's too late—his grades disqualify him from becoming an auror. Fortunately, curricular changes open more options for Harry, but not everyone is so lucky. Use your resources early in your college experience, and ask questions about anything you don't understand. If you are passionate about a career in Muggle Relations, you don't want to miss a required first-year course.

To learn more about career advising and testing for Harry and his friends, including some of the tests described in Chapters 1 and 2, you can read "'Have You Got What It Takes to Train Security Trolls?' Career Counseling for Wizards" (Kerewsky & Geiken, 2007).

externship, cooperative education placement, and *service-learning*) depending on your human services program's and school's structure and theoretical base, your developmental point in your program, whether you are an admitted major or community education student, your role and the services which you will observe or engage in during your placement, and other factors. Your first, and most important, consideration in choosing a site placement is that it fulfills all of the criteria required by your program and will count toward your graduation. This administrative consideration is critical—you can do the best, most meaningful placement in the world, but if your program doesn't recognize it, it will not move you toward graduation.

Site Placement Basics

Your placements are a very important part of your development as a human services professional. Be sure that you are aware of and familiar with your program's site placement requirements. Good questions to ask as you read your handbook and other materials include the following:

+ How many placements are required?
+ How many are optionally available to me if I want to do more than the minimum my program requires?
+ If I do extra placements, can I receive academic credit for them?
+ When in the program are placements completed (e.g., in which terms)?
+ Are there prerequisites to complete before I am allowed to start a placement (e.g., a required training on ethics and mandatory reporting, or admission to the major)?

- Is there a sequence of placements (e.g., a basic practicum that must be taken before an advanced internship)?
- Are there population-based placement requirements (e.g., a requirement for at least one placement with children/adolescents and one with adults)?
- Are there competency-based placement requirements (e.g., a requirement for at least one placement where you use a client case management database or learn about grant writing)?
- How can I learn which placements are currently available?
- How and when do I obtain permission from my program to apply?
- How and when do I apply?
- What deadlines and documentation are associated with obtaining a placement?
- What should I do if I am having trouble finding or securing a placement?

Your academic advisors and placement coordinator will also be able to help you find answers to these questions.

You may have additional questions related to your particular circumstances as well. These may include the following:

- Are there placements within walking distance of campus? Of my house? Placements on the bus line?
- I volunteered at a site. May I engage in a program placement there?
- May I be paid for my time at the placement? (For many programs the answer is no, but it doesn't hurt to ask.)
- Does the site have child care and am I eligible to use it?
- Can my differences, disabilities, or physical/cognitive challenges be reasonably accommodated by the site?
- Will my misdemeanor or felony convictions be a barrier to a placement at this site?
- Do I have special skills and abilities that may be useful at the site (such as fluency in Spanish or American Sign Language)?

These questions, which may be more individual or private, probably will not be answered in your handbook and will require consultation with your program.

Be Strategic About Your Field Placements

To be strategic and get the most from your placements, you can start by considering your current long-term career goals. Even if you do not have a specific career in mind, you may have some preferences that will narrow down your choices. This can be helpful if your program offers a wide range of opportunities. Do you have a specific goal, such as becoming an adoptions case worker? Starting with that goal, you can work backward to develop a sequence of placements (and classes or other training) that should lead logically to meeting the training requirements and competencies needed for that position.

- What are the requirements for this job? Find job announcements or use your career center's resources to find a list of common entry-level requirements.
- Make a chart so you can separate or break down each requirement.
- Identify at least one way that you can meet each requirement. After you develop your list, it may be useful to reorganize these items from the most basic to the most complex, or those that need to happen earlier or later in your process. This will help you to sequence your classes, placements, and other considerations, such as prerequisites or more extensive background checks.
- Highlight the components that you can meet through your choice of site placements. You may want to color-code these to highlight them, or color-code the requirements you hope to meet through site placements versus classes.
- Look at the components related to your preferred site placements. Are there additional considerations you should note on your chart? For example, if your program requires passing a language test before conducting services in Spanish, you will want to be sure to complete that requirement before you apply for a site where you will work in Spanish. You will need to allow enough time for this to be sure you meet the qualification before it is time to apply for the placement.
- You may need to extract potential requirements from the job description. For example, if the ad describes a job responsibility as "provide case management and related services including coordination of services," you will want to be able to explain your experience coordinating client services, even if you did so in an agency serving a different population.

As an example, here is a composite online ad from a search for "adoption case manager":

> New Namaste Children's Services is a private company providing international adoptions services. Our Colorado office seeks motivated individuals to work with a team to provide case management and related services including coordination of services, serving as point of contact for assigned families and associated agencies, participation in case planning and management, parent education and training, home visits, community referrals, and other responsibilities. All positions require a bachelor's degree in human services, psychology, or a directly related field from an accredited college or university. Must pass all drug tests and background checks. Must possess a valid U.S. driver's license. Some positions require a current passport. Preferred applicant characteristics include second language fluency (Asian languages or Spanish), previous experience in case management and adoptions, QMHA-eligible (Colorado) and international experience.

See Figure 3.1 for a preliminary breakout of job requirements based on this job description, highlighting a new human services student's job-based site placement strategy. It may look intimidating, but remember that this is a way to make sure you are tracking all aspects of a typical target job.

Requirement	Way(s) to Meet Requirement	Notes/Considerations
• Bachelor's degree from accredited college	• B.A. in Human Services and Criminal Justice anticipated in June, 2020	• University is accredited • Track requirements on advising handout • Can I take HSCJ 410: Advanced Case Management next fall? • Is there an adoptions class? Can I do an individual study?
• QMHA-eligible	• ?	• Research Colorado QMHA requirements • Make chart to document
• Preferred: Passport	• Get passport (in time for international placement?)	• Look at requirements and timing online • Ask for fees for my next birthday present
• Preferred: International experience	• International child placement? Placement with new immigrants or refugees? • Spanish? • Asia?	• Make sure this counts toward program requirements • If not, okay to do in summer? • Options through college international placement office? • Deadlines? • Costs? Scholarships? • Requirements? Visas? Vaccinations? • Language class option for Asian languages at community college?
• Point of contact for families and agencies	• At 3rd practicum (if not at child or family sites) • Spanish?	• If not in child or adult practicum, talk to site placement coordinator to identify agencies for 3rd practicum
• Coordination of services • Preferred: Adoptions experience • Preferred: Case planning and management experience	• Child/youth practicum in adoptions • Spanish?	• Look at available adoptions sites • Talk with sites about doing a case management placement
• Community referrals • Home visits • Parent education and training	• Adult practicum with parents? • Spanish?	• Talk to site placement coordinator to identify agencies where I can get these experiences

FIGURE 3.1   Breaking Out Common Job Requirements. *(Continued)*

Requirement	Way(s) to Meet Requirement	Notes/Considerations
• Preferred: Language	• Take SPAN 245: Spanish Medical Terminology	• Prerequisite: C or higher in SPAN 220-221-222 • Take prereqs this year? • SPAN 245 offered winter term (classroom) or spring term (online)
• Other responsibilities	• Keep a running list of all of my professional activities	• Highlight my flexibility and transferable skills in job applications
• Team skills	• Demonstrate in classes and sites • Take PSYC 339: Group Dynamics • Participate in team manager skills training at current site	• Document in reference letters and descriptions of specific times I demonstrated this • Ask for documentation of this site training
• Motivation	• Demonstrate in classes and sites	• Document in reference letters and descriptions of specific times I demonstrated this
• Drug tests	• Continue sobriety	• Keep attending 12-Step meetings
• Background checks	• Passed FBI check for program	• Keep a copy for my records • When does it expire?
• Driver's license	• Active	• Renew in July, 2022

FIGURE 3.1 *(Continued)*

Other Site Considerations

Some people seem to know exactly what type of work they want. Even if you are not one of those people, you may find that although your goals are not yet clear, you do know what you *don't* want to do. You may not want to be a case manager. You may not enjoy working with very young children. You may not be sure what you want to do, but you do know that the idea of a 9–5 desk job depresses you.

You may have other considerations as well. If your family member is the director of the only addictions treatment facility in town, you might not be permitted to complete a site placement at that agency, or you may want to specialize in a different area of human services to avoid multiple-role conflicts. If you were responsible for your father's care while he was dying of multiple sclerosis, you may want to avoid medical or hospice settings. Or you may feel that you would need more training in order to be effective with certain populations, such as interpersonal violence offenders. This information about what you don't want to do is just as helpful as knowing what you do want to do.

Try making a 3-column list with the headings *YES, MAYBE,* and *NO.* Using a list of the site placements you could apply to at your current status in your program, quickly identify the placements you would, might, or definitely wouldn't want to do. You can color-code these if you find it helpful. After you have gone through the list, transfer them to your columns. Looking at each category, do you notice any themes or similarities? For example, you may notice that you are more drawn to work in a team and prefer not to have primarily individual or independent activities. Or you may find that you want to stick to experiences similar to those you've already had.

It is reasonable to pay attention to the activities you do not want to do. We do not all want the same job or have the same career interests. Distance from home, time away from your children, and other personal considerations are also important to include in your decision-making. Your academic program will make sure you have a range of basic site experiences that meet your program's academic, training, and ethical standards. In most programs, you will still have choices about where you go. However, if you discover that you are making your career decisions on the basis of fear, bias, unpleasant personal experiences, or lack of knowledge, you would be wise to consider talking with a counselor to resolve your issues, open up more options, and be available to a wider range of clients in your future career.

Using Site Placements to Explore the Field

Many students are attracted to human services majors because they value hands-on learning. You may be a kinesthetic learner who absorbs information by doing rather than reading or hearing, or you may know that you are skillful at working in direct service settings. You may also expect that gaining more supervised experience in the field with clients may improve your value as a new employee. For these reasons, site placements tend to be one of the most exciting and stimulating components of human services programs.

If you do not know what your career goals are and don't have strong preferences, it might be helpful to use some of the career exploration tools described in Chapter 2. Your program may require specialized tracks or give you a generalist human services option. Career exploration may help you to have a satisfying educational experience while also keeping your options open.

Another way to clarify your career trajectory is to explore different site placements. Programs that offer two or more beginning placements provide a wonderful opportunity to investigate different areas of career focus directly. If you are not sure where you want to go in human services, first use the YES, MAYBE, NO activity described above. Consider building a schedule of distinctly different site placements from your YES list so that you can explore a broad range of human services areas. Don't forget that your program may require certain types of sites! For example, a student in a program that requires three beginning site placements, of which one must be child-focused and one adult-focused, might decide to apply these sites from her YES list in order to gain exposure to distinct areas of human services practice:

+ Aide in a Kindergarten classroom for children with developmental delays

Human Services Internship Handbooks

Several available handbooks provide in-depth discussion, resources, and activities related to human services site placements. Each emphasizes different aspects of site experiences, so take a look at the tables of contents to find one that is a good fit for your needs.

- L. A. Alle-Corliss and R. M. Alle-Corliss: *Human Service Agencies: An Orientation to Fieldwork* (2nd ed.; 2005)
- B. Baird: *Internship, Practicum, and Field Placement Handbook* (7th ed.; 2016)
- P. M. Kiser: *The Human Services Internship: Getting the Most from Your Experience* (4th ed.; 2015)
- H. F. Sweitzer and M. A. King: *The Successful Internship: Personal, Professional, and Civic Development in Experiential Learning* (4th ed.; 2014)

- Group observer, meal assistant, and case management assistant at an adult AIDS service organization
- Assistant grant writer for an organization that trains service dogs

You might discover that you love what you are doing at your first placement. You can decide whether to pursue other options or to continue focusing on this area of practice in your subsequent placements. What matters most is that each site placement contributes to your exploration and goals.

Supervisors, Faculty, Staff, and Fellow Students Are Site Resources

Although you may be unfamiliar with your potential site placements, remember that your campus and site supervisors, program faculty and staff, and fellow students are likely to be more knowledgeable about local sites. Don't hesitate to ask if anyone is familiar with a site or can point out a placement that may be a good fit for you. The more your program and peers know about you and your interests, the easier it is for them to steer you in productive directions—so get to know people, and let them know you, too.

Be sure you operationalize any recommendations you receive. This means that when someone tells you about a great site that's perfect for you, you'll ask questions about what makes it a great site, and a great site for *you*. Remember that everyone does not want the same things from a site placement. Your peer might recommend a site because the supervisor there is very informal and nonintrusive, but you might want consistent training and a high degree of feedback. A faculty member might point out a site that is a good match for your research interests but isn't a good match for the populations you want to work with. A trainee at your current site may rave about his previous site, but you might not be attracted to a police ride-along placement. It is part of your job to be intentional about your placements. No matter where you go, you will learn something valuable about the field, yourself, and how you want to help people.

Other Opportunities to Explore the Field

Some human services programs and related majors, such as psychology or social work, may provide extensive supervised site placement experience. Others offer limited supervision, a lower number of site experiences or hours, or only optional field work. Since you want to practice in human services, it makes sense to get hands-on training and experience in addition to theory. It may even be possible to receive academic credit or fulfill academic requirements through additional or extracurricular site-based activities. Don't forget about international internships. Ask your international or study abroad office about experiential or service sites and what scholarships or other funding may be available.

Finding More Placement Opportunities

If your program offers a low number of site experiences, hours, or credits, ask your academic advisor if you can register for more. If your program offers only optional site experiences, be sure you register for these. If it offers no for-credit options, consider volunteering at an agency that also serves as a training site for undergraduates—you may receive the benefit of their training structure and supervision even if you aren't receiving credit or participating in a formal site placement.

Service-Learning Experiences

Some institutions offer service-learning opportunities. These may be associated with a class (such as an Inside-Out Prison Exchange Program® (2018) that includes classroom and field learning), community service (such as helping at-risk teens plant a community garden), alternative break programs (including both domestic and international experiential learning and voluntarism), and other possibilities.

Noncredit Experiences

Your program or school may also offer noncredit service and learning trips to other communities. For example, a human services program, its department, or the whole community college may partner with an organization like Courts for Kids (2018). Students participating in the program gain experience fundraising and may participate in noncredit learning about athletics as a resilience factor for youth, the culture of the community they will visit, and how to be a culturally sensitive volunteer. They then travel to another country and collaborate with a community, sometimes in conjunction with local Peace Corps volunteers, to build a basketball court while living in that community. Or a program might offer a faculty-led trip to visit agencies, schools, personnel, and government representatives in Mexico, or to meet with students in China or Cambodia and collaborate on a project.

Noncredit, volunteer activities demonstrate your interest and intentions. They can be described in terms of the transferrable skills you learned and used, and associated with your career goals. For example, you might relate that your volunteer activity as a literacy partner in local psychiatric facilities helped you become a more effective interventionist through familiarity with and comfort on a locked ward, improved interpersonal and listening skills, and exposure to diagnosis and treatment planning for people with chronic mental illness.

You can also work in the field while you are in school. This has the advantages of pay and a formal position, but the disadvantages of being a job rather than a training experience, lack of coordination with your academic schedule, and the possibility of discovering that you are now committed to a job you don't enjoy.

What to Do Now

Consider your current and upcoming commitments and schedule. If this is a good time for it, get involved now! If this is not a good time, when will you be able to engage in or build on your training opportunities? You may want to use tools such as pro and con lists, timelines, or flowcharts to explore your options and ways to make your schedule work effectively.

Professional Organizations and Conferences

Classes, site placements, volunteer activities, and jobs are not your only opportunities to learn, practice, and engage in the human services field strategically. Consider joining a local or national human services organization, such as the National Organization for Human Services (NOHS, n.d.). Student members of professional organizations receive many standard membership benefits, which may include access to a job board, newsletters or other publications, and opportunities to participate in local and national advocacy. In addition, students often receive a discount on conference registration and may be eligible for awards and scholarships. NOHS partners with Tau Upsilon Alpha National Organization for Human Services Honor Society (TUA, https://www.nationalhumanservices. org/tua), which is a good way to network and a resume builder.

Attend professional presentations and workshops in your community to get up-to-date information or training in your field. National presentations are a good setting for more extensive networking with potential employers, academic faculty, publishers, and conference organizers. Some conferences permit students to submit proposals for posters or presentations. If student submissions are permitted if a professional or faculty member is involved, you have the chance to develop your collegial relationship with your faculty or supervisors. Presenting your capstone project at a national professional conference is another great experience and resume item.

Cultivate Relationships With Faculty, Staff, Supervisors, Peers, Alumni/ae, and Students

Of course, you can nurture your professional relationships more informally as well. Try visiting your faculty during office hours to chat about your career goals or learn more about their career paths. Most faculty, supervisors, and staff members are happy to show you their resumes or CVs. (A curriculum vitae, or CV, is like an annotated resume that is longer and more descriptive). Try to attend optional and social events in your program and on site. The more people know who you are and the more they see your professionalism and engagement, the more likely they are to think of you when other opportunities arise.

Remember that your peers and program graduates are your future colleagues and employers! Don't neglect to cultivate helpful, genuine relationships in your student cohort or at events that include alumni/ae. Student or student-community clubs and other groups provide a nice venue for establishing these relationships.

Engage Fully and Challenge Yourself With Your Classes and Site Placements

You probably are a very busy person. It can be tempting to slack off in your academics and placement at times, but resist that urge! The last thing you want to do is to come to your program's or site's attention in a negative way. If you are overcommitted or under stress and can't manage to get things back on an even keel on your own, consider using your resources. These may include an academic advisor, an instructor, or a counselor; your boss or site supervisor; your family and friends; or others who may be able to help you by providing empathy and support, suggestions, or flexibility in your responsibilities. When you need a reference letter or apply for a job, you want to be the person who *communicated well and managed a stressful situation,* not the person who *skipped class a lot, didn't participate, then got angry and talked to me only after receiving a C- in my class.*

Look at Employment Ads

If you already have a good idea what job or type of work you want to get after your degree, start looking at ads for those jobs now. This will give you a good sense of the advertised responsibilities, benefits, salary range, hours, and opportunities for advancement. You will also notice which agencies hire frequently and keep your ears open for an explanation: Is this a growing organization, or does it have trouble retaining staff? When you are ready to apply for jobs, you will be better informed about the position and better able to ask questions if information is missing from the ad or seems very different from typical jobs of this type. If you find particular ads appealing, you may want to keep a list of these agencies or units so that when you are ready to apply, you will remember to contact them to inquire about the positions for which they usually hire.

If you're still exploring your potential career, employment ads can help you learn about typical jobs and responsibilities, typical salaries, and benefits. They can also surprise you with jobs you hadn't considered, or jobs you didn't even know existed. As one human services student exclaimed on learning about a perfect classroom support position at a school for LGBTQ students, "I didn't even know this was a thing!" You might discover your life's work in a three-sentence ad!

Identify and Reduce Potential Obstacles

Now is the time to take care of potential obstacles to employment, because if you wait, you will be busy doing a capstone project, taking comprehensive exams, finishing your last college algebra class, or graduating. Or things might be going well for you now, but we do not know what the future will bring. Starting early gives you plenty of time to make your transition from school to career as smooth as possible.

If you have items on your background check that could be sealed or expunged, try to do so as early in your program as possible. As a bonus, successfully clearing your record may open more site placements to you. Is your ex racking up debt on a joint credit card? Have you defaulted on a loan? Failed to pay a fee that keeps you from accessing your transcript? Have you kept putting off required physical education classes? Do you need to finish a paper in order to keep an Incomplete from becoming an F? Have you lost your housing? Is your father's dementia getting worse? Human services faculty and staff often are well-informed about your campus's and community's human services resources and can point you toward the offices that can help you decrease barriers to your success.

Groom Your Public Presence

You may still see yourself as just a student, or you may be thinking that you have plenty of time before you apply for jobs. However, you should assess and, if necessary, clean up your public presence as early as possible. This includes evaluating your social media and online activity as if you were an employer, supervisor, client, or parent of a client. Log out of your social media accounts, then look at them from a public view. Your Facebook profile picture and name are always public, so make sure they are appropriate. You may be pleased with that vacation photo of you in a bikini drinking a margarita, but keeping it as your profile picture may not be your best professional decision. You may live in a state with legal medical marijuana, but a drawing of a marijuana leaf is not a good choice for your online avatar.

As noted above, seal or expunge any legal records if possible. If it is not possible, develop ways to explain or clarify these charges and describe why you are a good candidate for a job.

Start or Update Your Professional Portfolio

Your career center, program faculty, or knowledgeable peers can help you start collecting and organizing materials for your portfolio. Some workbooks and online resources include links or DVDs with templates and examples. Your career center may offer online or digital resources as well.

As a general rule, consider creating both a resume, which is a very brief summary of your education and work experiences, and a CV, which is a more descriptive and extensive document. Why both? Because different employers want different documentation of your experience. You may find that a book, website, or career counselor insists that you

Resume vs. Curriculum Vitae (CV)

A resume provides a brief overview of your key work-related experience. It can be read quickly and thoroughly. However, it provides few details and may omit important aspects of your placements and previous employment.

Compare resume and CV versions of the same position:

Resume

2016–2017   Intern, Guidance Office, *American International Institute,* Gabarone, Botswana

CV

2016–2017   Intern, Guidance Office, *American International Institute,* Gabarone, Botswana

Supervisor: Daniel Mogotsi, MSW (1 hour weekly face-to-face supervision)

Provided academic and social support for K–8 students through the Guidance Office of a US-accredited K–12 international school. Responsibilities included working closely with the guidance counselor to prepare orientation materials, collecting mid-year and end-of-year student performance data, offering TESOL preparation practice, observing students in the classroom, assessing academic placement level, and coordinating lockdown drills. Advised middle school honors service club and helped student editors prepare a quarterly online bulletin. Languages of intervention were English and Setswana. Students served by the office were from 34 countries and spoke 26 languages. Students represented a range of nationalities, cultures, and socioeconomic groups.

document your experience in a very specific way. It may be a good model, but it is not true that there is only one acceptable way to write a resume or CV, or that "all employers want a resume" or "you'll only get a job if you submit a CV." You can ask potential employers whether they prefer a particular format, and attune your materials to their description. If you have up-to-date versions of both, you will be able to do this efficiently.

Your portfolio will include more than your resume and CV. You may have standing letters of reference, copies of your previous diplomas and unofficial transcripts, letters of thanks or commendation, awards and honors, relevant publications, a spreadsheet of your work and training hours, articles documenting your professional activities or voluntarism, a summary of your capstone project, and other forms of documentation that demonstrate your professional skills and engagement.

Your portfolio may be digital or on paper. You may want to prepare and update it in both formats. Whatever you choose to do, start collecting materials and writing your resume and CV now. You will be glad you did when you learn about a great job with an application that is due in five days.

Be Flexible

Finally, be flexible where you can. It is strategic to develop a plan, and it is strategic to change the plan as your circumstances and interests change. For example, you may be very certain that you want to work with children, not adults. Your program requires an adult site placement, so you decide to get it out of the way first, choosing a site that provides housing and support for homeless parents and their children. You discover that it is difficult to intervene successfully with the children if their parents don't value and aren't part of the intervention. Your first love is still working with the children, but you realize that learning more about the parents will make you a more effective human services professional. Therefore, instead of the after-school youth athletics placement you were sure you'd do next, you decide on a placement that provides multiple services to families where a parent has been convicted of a drug-related offense. You will be working with the child and adolescent group program, but you arrange to attend the multidisciplinary case planning meetings with the psychologists and social workers who work with the parents. Where will you go for your third placement? How have your career goals changed, and in what areas are they still the same?

It is useful to map out a few logical sets or sequences of placements based on your learning goals, the opportunities they provide and their areas of training, and other factors. If your program includes a capstone project requirement or option, return periodically to the question of what you may want to your focus to be. Your program faculty, academic advisors, other staff, and students can help you balance your goals and outcomes with the high possibility of minor or major changes.

Chapter 4

Career Areas and Roles in Human Services

Career Options in Human Services

The expansive field of human services offers a multitude of areas of career focus and many different types of work. This variety is both wonderful and potentially confusing. This chapter provides an overview of some broad contemporary human services settings and job roles for people with associate's and bachelor's degrees in this and related fields.

Career Development

Maybe you know, and have always known, that your goal is to become the senior quality assurance officer for your county's outpatient child and adolescent health and wellness center. Or maybe you were sure that you would get a master's degree and become a family therapist, but your field placement at a research institute has made you fall in love with being a research assistant who conducts family intakes for studies or codes parent-child transactional data. And maybe you may have described your future career as "I'm going to work in human services!," but you're still not sure what that will look like. No matter how certain you are of your career path, or how overwhelmed you are with choices, the ideas in the previous chapters should have helped you take your first steps toward confirming, or narrowing down, the types of career areas and roles that are a good fit for your interests, training, and skills.

No matter what you want to do for work, you will go through stages of career interest and development that probably parallel your personal development and life circumstances (e.g., Ginzberg, Ginsburg, Axelrad, & Herma, 1951; Lent, Brown & Hackett, 1994, 2000; Super, 1980). Your first job probably won't be your only one, and it almost certainly won't be the job you still have at the end of a long career. You may not even be in the same field (Super, 1980)! A job or role you thought you would enjoy may turn out to be a poor fit for you. Workplace restructuring, moving to a new city, having children, a family illness, acquiring a license or certification, learning new skills, developing new interests, your own maturational processes, and changes in technology and the field are just some of the many influences on the path your career will take. This is a good reason not to agonize too much about your early human services positions. It is also a great incentive for continuing to describe your own skills and characteristics in ways that show how they apply to different kinds of work.

Over time, you may see patterns emerging in your human services career. These patterns can help you to decide whether to remain on this trajectory and improve your qualifications for more sophisticated or higher-paying jobs. They can also help you to become aware of repetitive work characteristics that are contributing to your job dissatisfaction, burnout, or unhappiness. Just as when you notice patterns in your personal relationships,

Side Box 4.1

Comparing and Contrasting Job Characteristics

An easy way to see patterns in your career trajectory is to look at your work history and group similar characteristics. You can do this in a several ways:

- Choose two of your previous or current jobs. They don't have to be human services positions, but it will be easier to see patterns that apply to your human services career exploration if they are. Think about one of your jobs. It may help to look at the job description. Write out some bullet points on its key characteristics. These can include responsibilities, areas of professional activity, skills used, and client characteristics, and also location, building maintenance, economic considerations, interpersonal issues, benefits, other positive and negative characteristics, and how you felt and what you thought about this job. Then do the same for the other job. Use a highlighter or colored pen to circle and connect the similarities. Do the same in a different color for the differences.

- You can add more jobs to this activity, and continue to mark the comparisons and contrasts.

- If you prefer, transfer your highlighted lists to a Venn diagram. Draw overlapping circles, one for each job. In the central, overlapping area, then write the features that two (or three, or more) jobs have in common. In each nonoverlapping circle, write the unique features of that job. This visual approach can make patterns more apparent.

- After you have a highlighted list or diagram of two or more jobs, identify the major patterns. Are there similarities or differences that you value? That you want in a job or want to avoid in a job? You can take your list of preferences to a career counselor, or use it for your own reference as you consider and apply for jobs.

you might decide that it's time to make a change. To give a fictional example, by the end of the novel *Other Women* (Alther, 1982), the protagonist Caroline realizes that her work as an emergency room nurse contributes to her unhappiness and negative world view, and takes steps to obtain a less stressful position, still within the medical field.

Using Your Holland (RIASEC) Code and Other Career Tests to Think About Your Career Development

If you have visited a career center or used online career resources, you may have completed the Self-Directed Search (SDS) and received your Holland Code. Your Holland Code can serve as an excellent shortcut for targeting your job exploration. Remember from Chapter 1 that the Holland Code is a summary of your self-reported work-related and hobby-related preferences and interests in six categories, and that the 6-letter code types have been linked with the jobs of people who have that code type and enjoy their work. Looking at the jobs listed for your type in the SDS materials and other resources that use Holland Code types is a quick way to identify a set of jobs that people with your type might find satisfying.

In addition to Holland Code and other testing results, it is useful to consider the degree to which a job emphasizes interpersonal interactions. Your preference for direct or indirect human services work may reflect your Myers-Briggs (MBTI®) type more than your Holland Code. Integrating your career testing results, your preferences, and the feedback you receive in your program and at field sites should help you productively in moving toward a job search and obtaining a position that is a good fit for you at this time.

It is helpful to think about your human services career as a trajectory or developmental progression (e.g., Landrum, 2009). You might have ideas about where it is going and where you want to get; or, you might only know that you need a job right now, and the one you see advertised is good enough. Sometimes your next job moves you toward a goal, and sometimes it is a good-enough job that meets needs other than career development. For example, a single parent with young children might pragmatically look for work that can be done online, or a job that provides child care, or a part-time position from 9:00 a.m. to 1:00 p.m.

Your job search and ideal versus good-enough jobs are explored in Chapter 6. This chapter briefly describes the kinds of human services jobs you may typically encounter. Of course, any job is likely to include a blend of job activities, responsibilities, and necessary skills. The term *client* is used below as shorthand for the many types of people who are the recipients or beneficiaries of human services activities. Where it is relevant, substitute *clientele, student, patient, soldier, employee,* or other more specific terms appropriate to the setting and role.

Direct Service

As the name implies, direct service jobs include working directly with people. For example, direct service positions could include activities such as welcoming clients or others to a facility, conducting screening and brief assessments, interviewing, determining case disposition, providing referrals, delivering interventions, leading psychoeducational groups, teaching or training, assisting other professionals, providing peer or professional behavioral support, supervising or managing personnel, evaluating personnel, coordinating services, making phone calls to arrange for services or resources, and similar responsibilities that involve working with clients, students, other professionals, and others.

Typical Characteristics of Direct Service Providers

Extraversion helps, but is not necessary, to be an effective direct service provider. The more you enjoy people or feel energized by them, the more chance there is that a direct service position will satisfy you and that you and your employer will experience it as a good fit. However, there is a great range of direct service job characteristics. Think about the difference between two jobs at a community college. One person is an interventionist who works individually with each adult student who is transitioning from military service to college. This takes place in an office with a door that closes. Down the hall, three direct services providers run an arts enrichment class for community children who are homeschooled. Today's class involves dancing to loud pop music and the children painting each other's faces. Today there are 12 children, but on any given day, 18 could show up. Shrieks of excitement bounce off the cinderblock walls as an argument erupts between two children who both want the green face paint. Both of these jobs are direct human service roles. Think about whether one, both, or neither is the type of job that you would enjoy.

Direct service roles require good interpersonal skills. This includes good listening skills and good communication skills. People who are successful in these roles must be able to build rapport quickly and convey warmth and empathy. They should be able to think on their feet, explain options, and confirm with clients that their needs are being met. They must have good organizational skills and be effective at helping clients receive services and navigate agency and community systems.

People using their services should feel that the direct service professional has understood their concerns and was able to provide some options. At the end of the encounter, they should feel that they have been listened to and treated respectfully, and that they understand the options that have been provided to them, even if they are not happy with those options or are still distressed or frustrated.

Direct Service Roles

Examples of direct human service roles include:

+ Case manager
+ Interventionist
+ Classroom aide
+ Supervisor
+ Youth coordinator

- Camp counselor
- Bilingual resident director
- Group leader
- Receptionist
- Screener
- Behavioral support specialist
- Peer recovery coach
- Staff trainer
- Resident services manager
- Greeter/information desk worker
- Consultant
- Liaison
- Coach
- Crisis hotline staffer
- Program director
- Program coordinator
- Prison reentry specialist
- Homeless camp outreach worker
- Needle exchange staff
- Resource specialist
- Counselor assistant
- Human rights advocate
- Spokesperson
- Consultant
- Testing coordinator
- Psychometrician
- Youth enrichment staff
- Pastoral or religious leader
- Residential staff
- Occupational therapy assistant
- Intake coordinator
- Childcare specialist
- Health care navigator
- Grief and loss interventionist
- Community developer
- Classroom autism specialist
- Elder social service coordinator
- International adoptions counselor
- Research assistant (some roles)
- EMT and other medical jobs (with additional qualifications)
- Teacher (possibly with other qualifications)
- Legal aide (possibly with other qualifications)

Notice that although these (and many other) direct service titles suggest that most of your time will be spent providing face-to-face or similar interpersonal services, all will include other activities as well.

The settings for direct service positions are numerous. They include online or remote interactions, nonprofit and for-profit agencies, preschools and universities, medical facilities, correctional settings, the military, governmental agencies, and more.

Indirect Service

Indirect service positions may still involve working with client information or providing services *for* clients or other people, but not directly *to* them. Think about the difference between direct and indirect job roles at a bookstore, for example. Cashiers, book shelvers, managers, and the person at the information desk all interact directly with customers. There may be people behind the scenes who are also providing at least some direct, interpersonal services, such as answering the phone, responding to emailed inquiries, training new staff, or interacting with delivery people. Others may have little to no interaction with customers or trainees. This might include an IT person who is at a corporate office, the contractor who writes advertising copy from her kitchen table, the accounts receivable clerk, the person unpacking boxes, and the cleaner who arrives at night and leaves before anyone else comes to work. Everyone may have a job that is a good fit for their preference for working with people or working with data, money, words, or objects. A customer will only interact regularly with the direct service staff, but those services rely on the work of the indirect service staff who are out of public view, accomplishing tasks primarily on their own, or interacting with a limited number of other peers to whom they are not providing services.

Typical Characteristics of Indirect Service Providers

People who are more introverted, or who enjoy working with a smaller number of people at a time, may prefer indirect service positions, but again, this is far from absolute. Successful indirect service providers still need people skills, but their positions tend to emphasize organizing data, writing, grant writing, manualizing, billing, documenting, developing advertising, technical or computer work, curriculum development, calculating, evaluating, reviewing, and similar tasks that support the organization's mission through infrastructure. These may include interpreting client materials or making recommendations based on testing, tracking, obtaining and dispersing funds, programming, and developing intervention or training materials.

Typical skills needed for these jobs include organizing, writing, tracking, and communicating. Jobs that are more individual may require strong self-motivation. Indirect positions may require more extensive technical and computer skills, the ability to work with databases, a good head for numbers, and the capacity to remember and keep track of many tasks and types of information. While direct service may be the most visible face of an organization, indirect service serves as the bones and a lot of the brain.

Indirect Service Roles

Examples of indirect human service roles include:

- Grant writer
- Administrative coordinator
- Project developer
- Content developer
- Quality assurance officer
- Case analyst
- Computerized test programmer
- Copywriter
- Advertising coordinator
- Event organizer
- Organizational manager
- Eligibility analyst
- Care coordinator
- Coordinator
- Human resources staff
- Patient tracking and management coordinator
- Board member
- Training developer
- Behind-the-scenes staff
- Research assistant (see below)

Indirect service settings include all of those listed above for direct service jobs. They may also work in larger settings, such as corporations, in greater numbers than direct service professionals.

Specialized Roles

In addition to the large categories of direct and indirect human service provision, three specialized areas are important to mention: research settings, international work, and jobs that may make use of human services training but do not typically appear in lists of human services positions. These roles may include direct and indirect service and may expand your thinking about job possibilities.

Research

In research and similar settings, there are many opportunities to use your human services degree. As a research assistant, you might be the person to deliver an intervention that is being studied, based on a manual or protocol. Or you might administer screening instruments, tests, or surveys, or watch and code video of interactions. In a different kind of project, you might calibrate and operate equipment measuring brain function, prepare or examine slides and samples, or help write articles and present results. Some research assistants engage in grant writing. Some work with the principal investigator (PI) to develop hypotheses and protocols for testing them, run statistical processes and model causal relationships, and document their findings as a small project associated with a large research project. If you are interested in learning more about research, ask your faculty about their work and whether student research assistantships are available at your institution. You might be able to earn academic credit while seeing if research is an area that works for you.

International Positions

Either during or after earning their degree, some people seek opportunities to work in another country. If you might want to do so, it is a good idea to talk with your academic advisor to learn whether international field placements, service-learning, or study abroad options are available through your school or can be integrated into your academic plan. Scholarships for international learning may be available. Outside your academic institution, you may find options to assist in medical missions, teach, or visit a country to engage in a noncredit internship. These are good ways to have a time-limited experience and see if international human services is a good choice for you.

Your career center or the office that coordinates job fairs can tell you whether international recruiters visit your campus, and provide some assurances about which employers they recommend. If you are interested in an international experience, start planning early, especially if you want to take language and culture classes during your degree.

Even after you have graduated, you may be able to apply for noncredit, postdegree international internships. These may serve as a first step in qualifying for positions that require previous international experience, or help you shift your area of work emphasis.

Related Positions

Some related job roles may also come to your attention. These may be positions within larger organizations that do not provide human services externally, but have internal positions that would utilize your skills. You might also discover that your human services training has prepared you well for other jobs that utilize your skill set. You might be the perfect fit for a bank's customer service department! Keep your eyes open for work that is not in human services but still may be an excellent match.

You may also find jobs that require a graduate degree. If a job appeals to you, keep track of that workplace's job announcements. They may have entry level positions as well. To learn more about the range of human services jobs at the master's and doctoral level, including many types of counseling and specialized intervention, take a look at books with an advanced focus, such as those by Burger, Youkeles, Malamet, Smith, and Guigno (2000); Collison and Garfield (1996); and Shally-Jensen (2015).

Other Considerations

Interests such as specific client populations, client ages, presenting issues, style or type of intervention, and similar considerations will also play a role in your job search. This

Refocusing Through a Postdegree International Internship

Pat graduated with a bachelor's degree in family development with a case management specialty area. After two years as a caseworker at the county jail, Pat wanted to work in a less hectic environment, with clients who were not moving rapidly in and out of the agency. Pat was also ready for a change of scenery after living in the same community for many years.

That spring, a friend spotted a small ad in a national newspaper and passed it on to Pat as a joke. The job was for a case manager at an agency serving elders in Scotland. Pat met some, but not all, of the qualifications.

Figuring there was nothing to lose, Pat applied for the position and was surprised to hear back from the director, Jo, within a week. The director said that Pat didn't meet the job requirements, but she wanted to discuss a different option. She was visiting her brother in a city near Pat, and asked if they could meet in a week. At the interview, she explained that she was a graduate of Pat's college (although she had been an international business major) and liked to hire alumni. Although the advertisement had been for a professional job, she also anticipated having two openings for interns at the same facility, beginning that fall. She was prepared to offer one of the internships to Pat, "Contingent on you taking a basic geropsych class that covers cognition and dementia up at the community college or online this summer. And maybe volunteer a few hours a week with the active seniors over at Snell Goodman Center. We can give them a call right now if you'd like. My brother is the volunteer coordinator. We could really use a case worker, but you'd be doing other work as well." She explained that the internship pay would be lower, but would include a room on the residential side of her agency, plus meals. Pat would need to apply for a passport and buy a plane ticket immediately, but Jo would take care of the internship employment paperwork on the Scottish side, and if Pat stayed for a year and completed the internship, the agency would reimburse the cost of the airfare. The internship could serve as a qualification for the professional positions. She gave Pat a copy of the internship contract to look over.

Pat's parents said, "Seize the day! Grandma Campbell was born in Glasgow!" Pat accepted the internship, completed a gerontology certificate at the community college, and moved to Scotland. Pat has continued to work in international settings and is considering future work in policy and infrastructure related to aging at a transnational organization.

is a good time to think about the kinds of clients and their needs that appeal to you. You will be able to explore how these client characteristics interact with the kinds of jobs that are available.

A Vague Job Announcement

Here is a fictionalized excerpt based closely on an actual human services ad from an online job board, with identifying details removed. What do you know after reading the description of the responsibilities associated with this job? What would you want to find out more about? Can you tell from the ad whether the job is a good fit for you?

- Support office infrastructure
- Provide economic desk responsibilities as assigned
- Support the support functions of this agency
- Assist in the determination of eligibility for benefits if needed
- Support local staff in supporting the work and the families using the case determination model
- Foster a welcoming environment for the public (over the telephone, in person in the lobby, at the counter, and by written correspondence)
- In a manner that preserves the dignity of the client, describe the programs and processes of the local resources

Most positions will include many different responsibilities. Only some of these will be listed in the position advertisement. Indeed, some job announcements are short on information (although others go into excruciating detail). Be sure that you ask about any tasks and activities that may not be evident from the posting.

Real People, Real Jobs

In the next chapter, real human services professionals talk about their work. If you would like to read additional stories from people in the field, see Shally-Jensen (2015), Landrum (2009), and the Career Stories at the VocBio Vocational Biographies site (n.d.) described in Chapter 1. You may also enjoy American Psychological Association's "How Did You Get That Job?" feature (American Psychological Association, 2018).

Chapter 5

Interviews With Human Services Students and Professionals

Career Trajectories in Human Services

What career paths do human services professionals follow? There are as many stories as there are people. In this chapter, you will learn about the careers of eight human services professionals. These are real accounts by real people, some of whom have chosen to share details of their professional lives, while others provide more general accounts of their career development.

As you will see from these human services professionals' stories, many roads lead to many different human services careers. As you read, look for areas where your own experience is similar to and different from their backgrounds, education, job choices, and passions. It may be helpful to pick at least one person whose career inspires you and identify similarities and differences in your path and theirs (Figure 5.1). Does this person's story help you think about your next steps or career direction?

First names or pseudonyms have been used by most of the interviewees. The exceptions are the professionals who operate their own businesses and agreed to have their full names and agency names included in this chapter.

Moira: A Current Human Services Student

Moira is a human services major and Japanese minor at a state university. She answered these questions at the end of her senior year. She is from Portland, Oregon, and enjoys reading autobiographies and snowboarding.

> Entering college, I had little to no idea what I wanted to major in, so at that point I had little concept as to what I would be doing postgraduation. As soon as I started working with adolescent girls, I knew that that is what I wanted to do long term, but the exact avenue for how I would like to do that is still unclear. I am looking into the Peace Corps but will likely take a year off before departing.

A site placement at a hospice helped Moira realize that this was not the right setting for her. Although she was disappointed, she used this experience

Choose an interview that interests or inspires you. Fill in the chart below, using one of your human services jobs or field site placements. Where are your experiences similar to or different from the interviewee's? Where does the interviewee's experience provide you with ideas or guidance for your own career search?

What other questions would you like to ask this interviewee or another person who has pursued this human services career path?

	Interviewee's Name:	Me
Experiences before bachelor's degree		
Site placements during bachelor's degree		
Other relevant experiences while earning the degree		
Career goals		
Jobs and career direction after graduation		
Vulnerabilities and needs		
Self-care activities		
Sources of encouragement and support		
Future goals and plans		

FIGURE 5.1   Comparing and Contrasting Career Trajectories.

to think carefully about her next placement. She says, "I was very fortunate that my very next internship was something that I was much more passionate about and ultimately realized that I wanted to do long term."

Moira's current site placement provides services for female-identified youth. Here is how she describes her responsibilities:

> I currently co-supervise an after-school drop-in program that provides a safe space and gender-specific services for girls age 10–18. This includes interacting with the girls in groups and one-on-one, establishing rapport, and becoming a trusted adult in their lives. In addition to this I also co-facilitate a 10-week girls' psychoeducational empowerment course that focuses on sexuality, sex, health, and self-love for girls between the ages of 14 and 18.

Moira's favorite aspect of this placement includes developing relationships with the girls. She likes hearing about their lives and experiences, noticing similarities and differences compared to her own adolescence. She notices that "there are several interns with a range of personalities, so it is really interesting to see which girls gravitate to whom and how special and influential those connections can be."

Moira is at the beginning of her career. She is interested in becoming more involved in research in the future, but her immediate goal is to complete her Peace Corps application.

Moira on Supervision

"Having the number of supervisors you do in my human services program definitely helped me figure out my professional goals. I was very lucky to have very strong and helpful supervisors at both my internship and at the university. This allowed me to bring any questions or concerns to experienced professionals and get opinions from someone at my internship and someone who has more experience in an academic setting."

Thinking about her own areas of potential vulnerability or difficulty in this field, Moira muses:

I have found it very important to be aware of the vulnerability in becoming too attached to an individual. While creating a bond with clients is important for building rapport, keeping a professional distance is also very important. This can be hard when the work is seemingly casual (sitting on couches with the girls talking, playing board games, eating a snack), and it is important for those lines not to get blurred. Additionally, while it is important to care for your clients in some capacity, the role that I am supposed to have is not a parental one. This can be a hard line to walk at times, especially if clients confide in you that they are going to make a bad decision. It helps me to remind myself why it is important to not take on a parental role, and to keep a professional distance.

Diane: A Community College Certificate Holder and Community Mental Health Provider

Diane was a first-generation college student. Her family did not even talk about college, and she did not think they could afford it. Diane also acknowledges that she was "a difficult teenager." She was a good student until she began working at age 16, attending school for half a day and holding two jobs. After some difficult early adult experiences and moves, she took a residential position on an East Coast horse farm.

Diane had previously volunteered at a psychiatric hospital, and working in this setting was her initial career goal.

When I was a volunteer, I was fascinated by the people I met, the complexity of their illnesses, and the degree of difficulty from which they navigated through life. I also saw things that frightened and sometimes sickened me. Abuse of power by some of the staff and doctors was still prevalent. This was in the 1980s, after deinstitutionalization and the movement toward community-based care.

Diane on Her Transition to Human Services

"After several years of riding racehorses in Virginia, I started to think about working in the mental health field again. I found a catalog for the nearest community college. They offered a certificate program in psychological services. I signed up for one class, loved it, loved the professors, and they seemed to like me. They encouraged me to pursue a career. I wasn't a great student in high school. I hung out with the wrong crowd. When I started college, it was like a light went on—I loved it! I couldn't wait to get to human services classes, and I loved the dialogue between students and the professors."

The use of Thorazine and newer antipsychotic medications sent people back into their communities. The ones who stayed were the people with intractable, serious mental illnesses. This is the population I found I loved working with—people with paranoid schizophrenia, bipolar disorder, and any kind of psychosis. I thought I would just volunteer at a hospital again, and maybe I'd have my foot in the door when I finished my education. I literally got the phone book out and started looking at psychiatric hospitals and making calls. Nobody seemed to want a volunteer, but one private hospital did want something called a "PRN Psychiatric Technician." I didn't even know what that meant, but I got myself an interview and was hired to work "as needed."

Diane worked overnight shifts and studied during the down time. Initially working with children and adolescents, she then filled in for a staff member on an adult acute unit. This experience reinforced her love of working with people with psychotic disorders. She worked on this unit for several years after earning her certificate, receiving an award for the outstanding care she provided.

When a part-time opening in community mental health opened, Diane applied. In her current position, she works under a federal grant as an outreach clinician with homeless people with serious mental illness or co-occurring substance abuse disorders. She uses motivational interviewing and works to build rapport and helping relationships with potential clients. Diane says she enjoys hearing their stories and making connections with many different people.

Diane notes that

I have to constantly challenge myself to keep learning. I work independently and find it's so important to staff cases with colleagues. My team consists of me and my partner, but I have many good connections with our outpatient therapists and doctors. Documentation requirements are constantly changing, and keeping up with this part of the job is a challenge.

Akiko: A Recent Human Services Graduate Working in a Nonprofit Agency

Akiko now works in school-based services at a nonprofit human services agency in the community where she born and raised, attended an immersive language school, and completed her bachelor's degree in family and human services. Of her current job she says, "As a woman of color who has lived here all of my life, doing the work that I do now gives me great joy in knowing that I get to be a resource for not only girls in my community, but specifically girls of color."

From the time she was in early middle school, Akiko knew that she wanted to work with teenage girls. She thought that she would be of the most service by becoming a psychologist or therapist, and initially wanted to start her own gender-specific practice. Therefore, when she graduated from high school and began her undergraduate degree, she immediately declared a psychology major. Here is what happened next:

> After my first college psychology course, I instantly realized that psychology was not for me. I spent a few weeks in utter panic that I had lost my way, until a friend of mine (who was a pre-major in family and human services) told me about a class called Exploring Family and Human Services. I registered for that class as an afterthought (and as something that would fulfill a general education requirement) and thought nothing of it. The next term, I walked into class and sat in the front row, and my life was forever changed. The way that the instructor talked about the major, what its values were, the work that it trained people to do, and the ways in which it taught people to be of service to others spoke to me on an incredibly deep level, and I knew that that program was where I was going to end up. That day I talked to the instructor about how to become a major. I took all the required prerequisite courses, applied, interviewed, was accepted, and the rest is history!

Side Box 5.3

How Akiko Found Her Job

"I was introduced to [my current job] through our required internship hours in the human services program. I interned here for two out of my three junior year terms and selected this organization as my senior site. After graduation, the agency received a grant to expand their school-based services. I applied and was offered the job. I've been here ever since!"

Akiko works as a school program coordinator. In this position, she oversees the scheduling, facilitating, and training of the agency's school-based services. These include girls' empowerment groups and classroom presentations. The agency also offers staff and parent education opportunities. School groups are available for girls from 5th to 12th grade. Girls meet with group leaders to discuss topics such as gender stereotypes, healthy relationships, social media, relational aggression, friendship boundaries, and related issues. The agency's classroom presentations are provided to all students in the class on topics including relationships, media and body image, conflict resolution, bullying, Internet safety, sexting, and sexual harassment.

Facilitating the groups gives Akiko the opportunity to meet and get to know girls in the community. Reflecting on what she enjoys about these groups, she says,

> Over the course of 10 weeks we share deeply, talk passionately, and really build a sense of community and support within our group. I love that I get to continue providing direct services and don't just sit at my desk all day. I actually play a part in the work that we do (and the work that I train others to do), but mostly, getting to spend time learning from and with girls is incredibly unique and inspiring.

Akiko's position requires organization, clear communication, flexibility, strong professional ethics, patience, assertiveness, public speaking, punctuality, and confidence. She explains some of the challenges associated with her work, including keeping within her scope of practice:

> Staying current on the information that we provide to students is definitely something I look out for. Making sure that we're providing accurate statistics on teen dating violence, sexting laws, and so forth is something I am always mindful of. However, the most important thing to remain mindful of is the information that girls share with me. Sometimes it's big disclosures or family issues, but regardless, it can be hard to hold all of that at times. Especially since I'm not a therapist. So, paying attention to the situations that call for a higher skill set than mine is key in being able to support the girls that I work with in the ways that they deserve.

Akiko loves her job and has a lot to say about why:

> I feel incredibly fortunate to work for an organization that so firmly believes in and encourages self-care. I work with 16 other amazing women who are so supportive and understanding and are always there to step in if I need to take some time to care for myself. Knowing that I can advocate for my emotional and mental well-being, and that I will be supported every step of the way, encourages me to take care of myself more often. I also see my therapist once a week (yay therapy!), so that also helps me to keep myself well and allows me to do the work that I do.

I would love to stay at my agency for as long as possible. I would like to obtain my master's degree at some point but am unsure about what I want to study or receive my degree in. Continuing to work with youth, particularly young girls, is where I feel my calling is, and is something that I'd like to be a lifelong endeavor. However, some of my personal dreams and goals, like expanding our family and having children, puts financial limits on my ability to remain working at a nonprofit organization due to financial reasons. So, in the long run, I know that I will not be here forever but will remain as long as humanly possible because I love this work more than I could have ever imagined.

Jade: Peace Corps Volunteer in Perú

Jade grew up on a tiny island off the coast of Washington State. After spending a term with Semester at Sea (2018) during 2015 and earning her bachelor's degree in human services, Jade applied for and began her Peace Corps experience. She presently lives in a community in Perú. She is interested in medicine and enjoys learning about the medical field. Her Peace Corps placement in the community health sector is a wonderful fit for her interests.

> When I first went to college I was hoping to be a nurse, and I still have this in mind for the future. Studying abroad on Semester at Sea cemented in my brain the idea that I wanted to serve as a Peace Corps volunteer right after college. Throughout college, I took Spanish language classes along with my human services curriculum, and interned at a medical clinic for low-income patients and Women, Infants, and Children (WIC). My college internships led me toward community health as a passion. I pursued my dreams and am currently serving in this sector. WIC really inspired me to my current and future path. I love working with women and infants/toddlers and hope to continue on this path after I finish my Peace Corps service.

Jade's Peace Corps service is varied and full. Here is how she describes her work, what she enjoys about it, and its challenges:

> I visit 30 moms monthly to teach sessions on nutrition, early childhood stimulation, and prevention of illnesses. I work closely with the health post [a rural health care facility] leading information sessions, working on wellness campaigns, and helping out in whatever other ways I can. I am also working with high school students to inspire them to be leaders in their community and encourage them in their futures. I help in the elementary school and taught an English class to elementary school students during their vacation. I have a lot of time on my hands, so I try to find side projects that have the potential to positively benefit the community as well. I also get to help out on my host family's farm, where we grow sugar cane and coffee among exotic fruits and other plants that flourish in a jungle-like climate.

Jade's Self-Care

> "As in any job, it is important to take breaks and practice self-care. I like reading, cooking, drawing, visiting other volunteers, and going to an internet café or a restaurant on occasion, though they are several hours away."

I love spending time with the moms, babies, and students, and just creating friendships with them. The cultural exchange is such an important part of my work, and I am grateful for our times together when we share stories and create lasting connections. I love playing with the kids, whether it is soccer, drawing, singing, or make-believe.

I am enjoying living out of my comfort zone and learning about a culture completely different from my own. The cultural differences can make work challenging sometimes. For example, the concept of time is less strict and punctual here than it was in the culture in which I was raised, so sometimes meetings start hours late or don't happen at all. I am practicing patience in my work and being open-minded to unexpected changes.

This position is a two-year commitment and then I will move on to a new job. I'm not sure where that will be yet. I am considering going back to school when I return, or potentially continuing to work abroad. I'm keeping an open mind.

Niki: From Nontraditional Student to Varied Human Services and Educational Practice

Like many people who find fulfilling careers in human services, Niki had a broad sense of what she wanted to do but was not sure where her specific interests and talents lay. Initially unsuccessful in her academic program, she found one of her many passions during a real-life community disaster:

When I graduated from high school in 1993, I immediately enrolled at the University of North Dakota in my hometown of Grand Forks. I wasn't sure what I wanted to be, but my parents insisted that I go straight to college and so that's what I did. I thought I might want to be a high school teacher or maybe a speech pathologist. But what I really wanted—what I really needed—was some freedom and autonomy in my life. It was a luxury I wasn't afforded in high school, having been raised in a pretty strict and sheltered household. So as a young adult with her first real taste of independence, I manifested it by "choosing" not to go to class if I didn't feel like it. And at that point in my life, it turns out that I didn't feel like going to class a lot. I was coming to the realization that I didn't want to teach high school and I didn't want to be a speech pathologist and, honestly, I didn't have any idea what I wanted to do. I was just taking random classes that met some general education requirements. After a couple of years of lackluster performance and being suspended and reinstated twice for poor academics, I ended up dropping out of UND with a cumulative GPA of less than 1.5.

Then in 1997, the town I had lived in my whole life experienced a catastrophic 500-year flood. The hotel I was working in at the time became the command center for the entire city. We housed FEMA, the American Red Cross, the Humane Society's rescue team, and all of the local city government offices. For the 6 weeks after that flood, I worked in conjunction with the emergency response teams. That was my first taste of crisis-related work and I loved it. I was good in crisis mode. I was finally beginning to incubate some tangible ideas about what I wanted to do with my life. In June of that year, I relocated to Oregon.

In Oregon, Niki found work that she both loved and struggled with. As a secretary in a substance abuse treatment agency, she liked the nonprofit environment, her colleagues, and the clients, some of whom were mandated to receive services. However, she found the agency's abstinence-focused, all-or-nothing approach to substance abuse treatment problematic and lacking in harm reduction education. She comments, "Although we were meeting the state requirements for the DUII program, we were doing our clients a disservice by not giving them skills that they could use once they completed our program."

She experienced a "career/educational epiphany" at 25 years old and reenrolled in school.

Side Box 5.5

Niki's Career Epiphany

"I decided I didn't want to spend my life doing clerical work and that if I wanted to change it, I needed to go back to school. With a lot of help and support and encouragement, I enrolled in a community college transfer degree program. This time, I was going to college because I wanted to—not because my parents were forcing me. This time, as I signed the FAFSA application as an independent adult, I realized that I was now financially responsible for my success or failure. Both of those factors were great motivators. I still wasn't sure exactly what I wanted to do, but it didn't really matter yet because I had a lot of clean up I had to do on my general requirements before I was going to be making any declarations of majors. But this time I had a plan."

Instead of enrolling in large lecture classes "where I was one of hundreds of faces," Niki chose small classes, where she made sure she interacted with her instructors so that if she was not in class, they would notice. She graduated with a very high GPA, including her difficult math classes, in about two years. When she applied to the state university, she received distressing news but persevered:

> When you graduate with a transfer degree, the premise is that you can then transfer directly to any of the state universities. I applied to one and was surprised when I received a letter from the admissions office informing me that despite my excellent community college grades, my cumulative GPA from both schools was still not high enough to meet their admissions standards. I had to write a letter petitioning for acceptance, acknowledging my awful grades and lack of effort, and promising that I was a different student now. It worked; they admitted me, but conditionally. I had to maintain a high enough GPA, and if I let it slide, I would be kicked out. But realizing that my poor choices were still haunting me 8 years after being kicked out of my first attempt at college was another motivator.

At the university, Niki met someone who had graduated from the human services program in its early years. Niki learned all about the program, including its use of a cohort model, emphasis on skills competencies, site placements, and job opportunities. She remembers, "It felt like I might have finally found the way to do all the things that I was good at—and get paid for it!" Niki was strategic about this program as well. Realizing that she would improve her chance of admission by doing so, she worked on meeting the program's prerequisites and the university's general education requirements.

> I made a point to get to know the instructors and to make sure they knew who I was. I was vocal during classes. I utilized office hours. I asked hard questions with the intention of stimulating rigorous debates. I took the information and education to heart.
>
> I also developed a core group of friends who became my regular study group companions as well as my regular group project/presentation people. I chose that group very intentionally. We were all from different backgrounds—ethnically and racially, ages, socioeconomic status, gender, sexual orientations, marital statuses, parenting choices, religions, languages spoken, and career history. This brought a tremendously varied breadth of voices and experiences to our conversations. We also all had very different skills sets with varying strengths and weaknesses. We supported each other, reassured each other, challenged each other, created self-care opportunities with each other, pushed each other, kept each other accountable, complemented each other, contrasted with each other, consoled each other, and congratulated each other.

Equally intentional about her choice of site placements, Niki explains her goals and steps toward achieving them:

> When I was in high school, I had somewhat inadvertently become a sex educator—mostly because growing up in North Dakota, very few people were willing to talk about sex in a comprehensive manner and there was a massive need, and because there wasn't much I was ever scared to talk about. I also had finally figured out the concept of harm reduction as it related to both risky sexual behaviors and drug and alcohol use. I knew I wanted to work in an agency that was focused on harm reduction and sex-positive education, and I found that exact agency. For another placement, I knew I wanted to work with queer-identified youth, but none of the established internship options available really fit the bill. Working with the program's site placement coordinator, I created my own internship working with a camp that served kids of LGBTQ parents one week and LGBTQIA2S [an umbrella term] youth the second week. With my final junior year placement, I again was able to create an internship where I could develop a campaign geared toward reducing intimate partner/ sexual violence. I then jumped at the chance to take part in an international educational opportunity with a group of human services students and staff in Mexico.

After graduating with honors, Niki was hired as a program coordinator at one of her placement sites, engaged in the sexual education and harm reduction work that had inspired her student choices.

> At the end of that job, I went to work for one of the local school districts as a family development specialist—a title they created to better describe the gamut of duties I had there. I was teaching toddler classes and parenting classes, offering a summer camp for high risk middle schoolers, and providing an after-school program for homeless, queer, and other disenfranchised teenagers. I had the opportunity to work with the Diversity and Equity Cadre on a district-wide level. After several years there, I was recruited to the high school by a principal who decided she wanted a visible, out, queer staff member centrally located in her school. I worked with youth at high risk of not graduating to help them meet their educational goals as well as help them develop employable work skills. While I was working for the school district, I took another part-time job with an agency that I had been volunteering with for years as a crisis counselor. I was also offered the opportunity to start teaching in the substance abuse prevention training program at the university. Eventually, I left the school district and started doing the crisis work full time and teaching part time. I had the opportunity to teach classes on bullying, teen suicide, and cultural identity development for 9 years. I also started a radio talk show about sex and served as a consultant to local agencies.

Niki's work with many people in distress has taught her a lot about her own vulnerabilities and triggers. She has learned that in order to be available to her clients and students, she needs to take care of herself. After a serious injury, Niki has taken care of herself by letting go of some of her many responsibilities, although she continues to volunteer as a crisis counselor and communications liaison. She hopes to increase her crisis work over time and to explore other human services roles. Asked whether she has considered additional education, she muses:

> I'm not sure if another degree is in my future, but I've never felt that I "settled" for just having my bachelor's. I have always said that the human services program I attended is one of the best platforms I could have gotten underneath me to qualify me to do all the things I wanted to do at the time. I feel just as well-equipped as many of my fellow students who went on to get their master's in social work or other related fields. I also completely believe in the old adage that you get out of the program what you put into it. There's no part of me that feels I didn't give my all to my program.

Rachel: From Human Services to Research and a Future PhD in Counseling Psychology

Unlike the other interviewees in this chapter, Rachel has enrolled in a graduate program. She received her bachelor's degree in human services, worked for several years in the field, then shifted her professional focus by working as a research assistant.

Rachel first thought that she might become an elementary school teacher. However, she found her human services classes more compelling. Her site placements were at a mentoring program for at-risk youth, a child abuse and neglect prevention program, and an agency serving families with children who are experiencing homelessness. At the latter placement, she was able to work with a case manager.

Throughout her undergraduate degree, Rachel remembers that

> as a first-generation college student, I often felt lost and questioned my abilities and whether or not I belonged in academia. However, the human services program did a wonderful job of supporting students and providing guidance along the way. Several professors took the time to acknowledge my work, provide guidance, and help me navigate future career decisions. As part of the program, students also met weekly in small groups with a doctoral student supervisor. This additional support and encouragement was really helpful.

After graduating, Rachel worked as a surgery scheduler with a surgical group that had employed her since she was a high school junior. She traveled and volunteered in India and Southeast Asia for half a year, then taught math and reading to 4- and 5-year-olds while working as a receptionist in a medical clinic. Her human services placements qualified her to work as a care coordinator for people living with HIV through an AIDS service organization for several years. Rachel became increasingly interested in attending graduate school.

Rachel on Navigating the Graduate School Application Process

"I grew up believing that people in my family didn't go to college. Upon graduation, many of my peers were applying to programs to get their master's degrees in social work. While I considered this route, I ultimately decided to work in the field first and return to graduate school later. While I was determined to engage in direct service work upon graduation, I was also considering graduate school. As a first-generation college student, however, I felt pretty lost when it came to how to navigate applying for (and more importantly how to pay for) graduate school. As it was, I wouldn't have gone to college if a friend of mine hadn't insisted that I complete an application (and had I not received grants and scholarships to support my academic endeavors)."

Rachel remembered hearing that no student from the undergraduate human services program had yet been admitted to the college's doctoral counseling psychology program and being told "maybe you'll be the first." She was. Her first attempts to enter a doctoral program were unsuccessful. On the advice of a mentor, she reached out to a faculty member to learn if she could volunteer through her research institute in order to gain experiences that would further qualify her for the doctoral programs that interested her. Rachel says that without her mentors, she would not be where she is today.

Of her two years as a research assistant, Rachel says, "Working as a research assistant not only equipped me with the research experience I needed to be a competitive candidate for graduate school, but it also solidified my passion for marrying research and clinical practice."

Rachel's current career goals include a variety of activities:

In my doctoral training thus far, my research has primarily focused on understanding the pathways to health-risking behaviors among adolescent girls with trauma histories, exploring ways in which to bolster resilience and prevent the deleterious effects that trauma can have across the lifespan. After obtaining a PhD, I hope to work in academia as a professor while continuing research on trauma prevention and interventions for adolescent and young adult populations. I am also very interested in working as a practicing psychologist alongside teaching and research, and am particularly interested in working with adolescent and young adult populations with a particular focus on girls and young women.

As a graduate student, Rachel now provides many of the mentoring roles that were so instrumental in her own success. She assists and co-instructs undergraduate human services classes, teaches, evaluates student work, provides academic support and guidance, helps advise undergraduate honors college theses, and provides university-wide training.

> As an instructor in the human services program from which I graduated, I have the unique opportunity to incorporate my lived experience into my lectures, drawing from my work as a case manager, research assistant, and international volunteer, including co-leading two groups of undergraduate students on service learning trips to Panama and Nicaragua with Courts for Kids (2018). I now have the opportunity to give back and serve as a mentor in a way that former professors served as a mentor for me. I get to engage in university-wide efforts to engage students in critical dialogue. I also have the opportunity to infuse elements of social justice and trauma-informed approaches into the lectures I deliver.

In her role as a human services instructor, Rachael is getting to see what the educational process looks like from the other side:

> I'm often teaching students who are coming in at very different developmental levels. For instance, there may be students who are very well-versed in issues pertaining to systemic bias (either through lived experience or past courses), and there may be students who don't believe systemic bias is real or have never thought about these issues. As an instructor, I have to balance providing baseline knowledge about certain content areas while also speaking to and challenging students for whom this information is not novel.

Rachel has learned that it is hard for her to do her work well if she is feeling depleted. Her self-care activities include yoga, meditation, therapy, gardening, backpacking, travel, and spending time with her partner, friends, and cats. She notes that it is important to protect your self-care time, acknowledge what you can and cannot do, and set healthy limits. She also recommends asking for support, guidance, and consultation from colleagues.

Following her adult and child/family practica, Rachel hopes to complete doctoral site placements at a state hospital and a clinic where she can learn to use ADHD and learning disability assessments. She hopes ultimately to practice as a psychologist, teach, and engage in research. Her focus is on people who have had traumatic experiences.

David Gardiepy: Program Coordinator of a Training and Education Organization

A gay, two spirit Native American, David overcame significant educational barriers and was the first in his family to graduate college. He earned a general studies bachelor's degree with minors in child development, marriage and family counseling, human services, and addiction, and holds a state Certified Alcohol and Drug Counselor certification (CADC II).

David's human services career began with an internship:

> After working as an intern in a facility that treated adjudicated individuals, I started employment working on an intensive community treatment service team with children who live with severe and persistent mental illness. From there, I began my bachelor's degree. While volunteering with NAMI [National Alliance on Mental Illness, 2018], I wrote a Peer Recovery Support Specialist training manual and presented at the 2016 NAMI national convention in Washington, DC. I also started working as a community trainer at a local university, which resulted in employment as an instructor. From there, I obtained employment as a substance abuse counselor.

David did not just learn how to work in these human services roles. He also observed how the organizations met their clients' needs: "I realized how inadequately prepared some counselors were for the positions they were hired for. This resulted in the creation of PACES [Psychological Assessment, Consultation, and Education Services, n.d.], with the goal of improving real world education." PACES provides chemical dependency certification training courses and continuing education on substance use disorders. David is a developer and the program coordinator. He credits the then-president of his state addiction counselor certification board and his adoptive mother for giving him the courage and support he needed to progress through his education and create PACES.

As lead developer, David provides supervision and approval of outside curriculum materials, interfaces with accreditation bodies, designs and maintains the organization's website, recruits participants, and engages in other tasks associated with growing and maintaining a business.

Side Box 5.7

David: "I Did Not Think That I Would Become an Educator"

"When I started attending a local community college I thought I would be able to obtain employment as a community resource provider, handing out food boxes and assessing individuals to see if they qualified for specific resource programs. I did not think that I would become an educator or travel the United States providing various presentations and trainings."

Asked what he likes about his work, David responds:

> I enjoy being able to work from home, while interfacing with accreditation
> bodies and credentialing bodies. I enjoy being able to choose whom I work
> with based on their professionalism and ability to act within ethical guidelines.
> I also enjoy knowing that my work is promoting an underrepresented field of
> employment and is actively working to improve counselors' knowledge.

In addition to his work with PACES, David takes care of several people over the age of 75. He prioritizes taking weekends off to spend time with his husband and pets, plant trees, advocate for the environment, and enjoy being in nature. Trips to Hawaii, for both work and pleasure, "have provided me plenty of opportunities to recharge and get ready for the next stages at work and in my career, as well as in my personal development." One of David's work responsibilities is to keep up with the fields in which PACES offers training and continuing education. He reviews PACES's materials to make sure that they are up to date and meet certification requirements. He would like to return to direct service at some time:

> This is a small resting spot. While I could conceivably stay where I am, I strongly
> desire to get back into clinical work. In the future, I anticipate completing my
> degrees and obtaining employment as a co-occurring disorder therapist, as well
> as a family systems therapist. I have many lofty goals in life, and I fully intend
> to meet all of them while surpassing the expectations placed on me by family.
> I have already beat the statistical societal norms as I have maintained a lawful
> existence, all the while knowing that my upbringing and life situations could
> have easily led to a life of crime and addiction.

Bhavia Wagner: Building an International Organization From Scratch

The last interview in this chapter is with the person who made the most radical career shift from her undergraduate major to a human services career. Bhavia earned a bachelor's degree in environmental education. Today, she is the executive director of Friendship with Cambodia, a U.S.-based international nongovernmental organization (NGO) providing humanitarian aid to vulnerable people in Cambodia.

Bhavia always had a strong affinity for environmental causes, volunteering for local actions in middle and high school. She was also politically involved, serving as the youngest member of the local chapter of the League of Women Voters when she was 17. She jokes, "I guess I was born with activism in my blood." However, her early career was environmentally focused. She became executive director of a watershed council in Northern Michigan, "a part-time position without benefits in a remote area" that "combined my interest in nature with my inclination toward advocacy." Looking back, she comments that "I didn't know it at the time, but the rest of my life would be spent as the executive director at various small nonprofits." In this position, she learned many of the tasks associated with nonprofit management, including creating programs, public speaking, fundraising, writing for newsletters and websites, managing finances, creating budgets and strategic plans, and working with a board of directors as well as volunteers, staff, and donors. As the organization grew, she was able to hire specialized staff to take on some of these responsibilities. Bhavia realized that

> at that point, it wasn't as much fun for me; I had become the administrator. I realized that creating an organization was what I enjoyed, much more than maintaining it. One of the lowest points was when I let someone go. Personnel management was the hardest part. It had been a wonderful job, but I felt ready to move on.

She moved to California and found a job as the part-time director of a peace center. She was again the only employee, bearing all of the responsibilities in the organization.

> The organization's members were still in the mindset of protesting war. I wanted the organization to be more proactive for peace, so I helped them start a Raising Peaceful Children education program for the parents of preschoolers and a Teaching Tolerance program in local high schools. It was the creativity of building an organization that really engaged me. I also enjoyed working with the volunteers and donors. It was more challenging to fundraise for a peace organization, but it was satisfying to help it transition from an organization with a founder/director to one that could keep going with hired staff.

Bhavia remembers an important visit to a friend who was a Peace Corps volunteer in Liberia as "one of the most transformational experiences of my life." Living in the village with her friend, she "really had a hard time reconciling in my mind the poverty that these people experienced and the luxurious lifestyles and opportunities we have in the West. It disturbed me so much that it took about a year before I could talk about my experience."

> A few years later, I took a summer off and went to Spanish language school in Quetzaltenango, Guatemala. While I was there, in 1989, I learned about the horrifying human rights abuses against college students and indigenous people by the CIA-backed Guatemalan military government's counterinsurgency operations. When I returned to the United States, I started volunteering for an organization focused on human rights in Central America. It was the beginning of my international work.
>
> At this point in my life, I had visited a country in Africa and a country in Latin America. Now I wanted to visit a country in Asia, but only if the trip had some higher purpose than just being a tourist. When I heard about the Peace Walk in Vietnam, a citizen's diplomacy effort at a time when the United States had not normalized relations with Vietnam, I knew wanted to be part of that delegation. It had been 15 years since the Vietnam War ended, but the U.S. government was still imposing a trade embargo.

The trip to Vietnam was "amazing." At the end of the tour,

> twelve of us hired a van and drove from Ho Chi Minh City to the Combodian capital city of Phnom Penh. The streets of Phnom Penh were practically deserted, except for some barefoot children dressed in rags. There were no passenger cars, only a few cargo trucks. It was 11 years after the genocide ended, but I could see that people were still traumatized. The vendors in the market had blank looks on their faces. The U.S. government had convinced the United Nations to block international aid to Cambodia, because of Cambodia's alliance with Vietnam. Recovery was very slow.
>
> I had seen poverty in Africa and in Latin America, but the poverty I witnessed in Cambodia was far worse. Besides being extremely poor, the people were psychologically shattered. I decided that Cambodia needed our help, and I would do what I could. What could I do? Drawing on my organizing skills, I decided to lead tours to Vietnam and Cambodia, to take Americans over to witness what I had seen. Maybe some of them would be able to help.

She began leading tours and receiving requests for help from local people. For example, a group of women asked for help starting a microcredit program. She presented these requests in the United States during educational programs based on her trips. This resulted not only in donations but also inspired audience members to start their own programs.

Side Box 5.8

Bhavia in Cambodia

"In Cambodia, I started working with women's organizations, trying to help them market their handicrafts in the United States. I was very touched by the people I met. They had experienced enormous suffering during the genocide, yet they had the resilience to rebuild their lives and maintain their kindness. The strength and goodness of the human spirit shone through them. I stayed for three months and interviewed 14 genocide survivors for a book I wrote, *Soul Survivors: Stories of Women and Children in Cambodia* [Wagner & DuBasky, 2002]."

After her book was published, she began touring nationally to present on Cambodia. She made contact with people in numerous cities and decided to start her own organization, Friendship with Cambodia. Since 2003, we have given over $1.6 million in humanitarian aid to Cambodia. We partner with local organizations in Cambodia. Our programs include support for poor rural students to attend university, women's self-help and savings groups, a shelter for street children, a recovery program for trafficked girls, and a program to help women disabled by landmines. Our main goal is to empower people to help themselves, through education and microcredit. We focus on women and girls because they are more disadvantaged, and because the research shows that helping women and girls is a key factor in ending family and community poverty.

In 2010, Friendship with Cambodia published a travel guide to Cambodia, now in its second edition, emphasizing tourist options for responsible and ethical travel (Mayeda & Friendship with Cambodia, 2017).

Although she enjoys the start-up process, Bhavia characterizes starting Friendship with Cambodia as "my most challenging career undertaking."

> The gratification of being able to help people in need has made it worth the effort. I still cry when I see the photos and read the biographies of the women and children we are helping. They have such difficult lives. Working too hard and getting burned out has been my greatest challenge. I find I need to take time off and get away for some recovery time.
>
> I used to imagine that the organization would grow bigger and I would move on to my next job. But that never happened. Now I feel content to stay and just enjoy my work. It offers opportunities for creativity and lots of variety, and is full of meaning and purpose. I have developed many nice relationships with our volunteers, donors, and staff in the United States and Cambodia. I am 61 years old and hope I can continue working at Friendship with Cambodia until I retire.

Bhavia still makes time to help other nonprofits get started, as a volunteer consultant. She reflects, "I am glad that I can share methods that have worked for me. It is a joy to help others."

Thinking about Human Services: The Interviews and Beyond

These questions and activities are a starting point for your deeper consideration of your human services trajectory:

+ If you found yourself in a situation similar to Niki's description of her early academic experiences, what could you do and which resources could you use to get back on track?
+ Which of these jobs would you enjoy? What aspects of each job make them potentially enjoyable for you?
+ Have a conversation with a classmate who would enjoy different jobs. Help each other to articulate the aspects of each job that appeal to each of you.

- As you read these interviews and used the worksheet (Figure 5.1) to compare and contrast your experiences with one or more interviewees', what insights emerged about your own career experiences and career path?
- If you completed the worksheet for an interviewee whose story interests or inspires you, complete it again for an interview that was less similar to yourself, or less engaging. What similarities and differences do you see when you compare your experience with this person's?
- Complete the worksheet again, this time comparing yourself to the person whose story is least like yours. What can you learn about your own career preferences by looking at a career trajectory and outcomes that are very different from your own?
- Can you guess each interviewee's possible Holland Code type? For example, David and Bhavia both developed successful human services organizations. What would you guess is their first RIASEC letter? Jade is living in a Peruvian village and providing direct service. What might her first code letter be?
- See if you can write a job announcement for each interviewee's current role. Include these required and preferred qualifications:

  - Education
  - Licenses, certificates, or other credentials
  - Skills and competencies
  - Major job responsibilities and tasks
  - Other job characteristics (e.g., legal constraints, eligibility, schedule, or location)
  - Personal attributes (personality; preferences; and MBTI®, Big Five, FIRO-B®, and other career-related normative information)
  - Experience or background

- What interview questions might each of the interviewees been asked?
- Think about the human services classes you have taken, or will take. Which classes would help prepare you for each of these jobs? Are there additional classes that would enhance your application for one of these positions?
- Similarly, are there field site experiences, volunteer roles, or other service opportunities that would improve your fit for each job?
- Consider the interview that describes your least-good fit at this time. Write or talk with a friend, classmate, or career counselor about what factors contribute to the poor fit. Based on this exploration, write a description of yourself and your career goals that is phrased positively. For example, if you would rather leave the field than have to work with adults, you could say, *I have a strong preference for direct service work with children.*
- Use these interviews and the sources of vocational stories described in Chapters 1 and 2 to identify a few types of jobs that excite you.
- Work with your career center, academic advisor, and others to find people in your area with these and similar jobs.

- Contact at least one of the people holding these jobs and ask if you can talk with them about their work. (Hint: Offer to take them out for tea or coffee, or to meet them at their workplace.)
- You may be able to shadow someone at their job (depending on their permission, confidentiality, and other considerations).
- Interview your peers who have field site placements that appeal to you and seem like stepping stones for your career goals.
- Don't be afraid to ask people if they will tell you about their jobs! Most people are pleased by your interest and will help you if they have the time. If someone isn't able to talk with you or allow you to shadow their day, ask another person. Keep trying until you find someone to connect with so that you will have as much information as possible about that job.

Common and Differing Elements of the Interviews

In the eight interviews in this chapter, you probably noticed similarities that are evident across several people's experiences, as well as some differences. For example, most of these interviewees have found work they love after completing a bachelor's degree, and some have associate's degrees or certificates. While some are considering graduate degrees, most are satisfied with the jobs they found after completing their undergraduate degrees. Several have international experiences, and all have had domestic site placements or jobs. Some knew exactly what type of work they wanted, and others shifted course. Some found that, in retrospect, there were clues that pointed them toward human services professions. Some work well alone; others prefer a team approach. Everyone wants to be helpful to other people, which some interviewees do through direct service, while others teach, write, and work in administrative roles.

This is good news! There is no wrong path to a fulfilling human services career. These stories should increase your confidence that you will find jobs that are right for you.

Chapter 6

Your Job Search

B y now, you should be familiar with the human services field, the major types of human services jobs, and your own preferences and skills. This chapter looks at some of the nuts and bolts of the job search, as well as resources to support you in finding and applying to jobs that meet your current needs, whether they are pragmatic ("I just need a job in the field!") or ideal ("I want to provide support and case management to foster parents of babies 0–2 years old"). It also includes suggestions for improving your written materials, interview skills, and qualifications.

If you are not yet at this point, or need a general overview of the job search and your materials before reading this chapter, take a look at guidebooks such as *What Color Is Your Parachute? 2019: A Practical Manual for Job-Hunters and Career-Changers* (Bolles, 2018), or those for related fields, such as *Finding Jobs with a Psychology Bachelor's Degree: Expert Advice for Launching Your Career* (Landrum, 2009). Your library or local career center should have a variety of books and workbooks on this subject, including less-familiar career routes such as starting your own business; military jobs; or working internationally in educational settings, the Peace Corps, or a charitable organization.

Resources for Your Job Search

Where will you start your job search? There are many resources and strategies—what matters is determining which will work best for you. Explore your options on your own or with your classmates, but remember that what works for you may not be right for your friends. You can help each other out and provide support for your future colleagues.

Finding Jobs

By this point in your career exploration, you should be familiar with your institution's career center. If you haven't yet visited and talked with a career counselor, now is a great time, especially if you are not yet seriously beginning your search. The career center's resources may help you narrow down or expand the range of jobs that interest you, and you will be able to get an overview of the services and resources while you are relaxed and not under time pressure.

Some smaller schools do not have career centers. If your school does not, check with your local community college. Local government sometimes offers limited career services as well. Don't forget that you may be eligible for some of the services at your local human services agencies. If your community publishes a social services directory in print or online, review the headings to see if you qualify to use community agency resources for preparing your materials and your job search.

Finding Job Announcements

Human services jobs are advertised in a variety of places and media. These include print and online newspapers, online job boards or job announcement lists, governmental or agency-specific websites, paper flyers on bulletin boards, recruitment visits in your classroom, email lists, on- and off-campus job fairs, ads in print and online professional publications, and announcements from NOHS and other professional organizations of which you are a member. Some agencies advertise on Facebook or other social media. You may hear about a position from a supervisor or classmate.

You can also contact potential employers directly to ask where they announce openings or to learn whether they maintain an applicant pool for temporary workers. Ask whether they use any standard forms or application materials that you could receive and complete now to speed up an application later. If you are not sure where an agency advertises, ask them. Some only list openings on their own websites or email lists.

The number of different ways jobs are posted may seem overwhelming. Remember that no employer will use all of these methods. However, if you are in an active job search, it will be helpful to make a weekly list for yourself so that you will remember to consistently (but not obsessively!) check the sites, lists, or organizations you have targeted. For jobs that appeal to you, keep track of the information with a checklist (Figure 6.1).

Put Yourself Out There!

You can also advertise yourself in a variety of ways. This is a scary proposition for some people who are less experienced or less sure of themselves, more introverted, or from cultural groups where praising or promoting yourself is considered rude. If you are not comfortable articulating a realistic description of both your strengths and areas for improvement, consider discussing this with a classmate, your faculty or staff, a counselor or career counselor, or a consultant from your cultural group who can help you to show your gifts to a potential employer in a way that is bridges your culture and the culture of that workplace.

Promoting Yourself Through Professional Behavior

Remember that as a human services student, you are a professional in training. Among other things, this means that your faculty, staff, supervisors, coworkers, and classmates are already noticing whether you behave professionally, ethically, and legally. This is

Site or entity	Where	May 1	May 8	May 15	Notes
FBI	www.fbijobs.gov	✔	—	✔	✔ Set up acct
Las Vegas (Firefighter)	https://www.government-jobs.com/careers/lasvegas?	✔	✔	✔	
Craigslist (Las Vegas)	https://lasvegas.craigslist.org/search/jjj	—	✔	—	Filter government, healthcare, human resource + non-profit + full-time
Las Vegas Review-Journal	https://jobs.reviewjournal.com/	✔	—	—	Check on June 1
Lucy's father Jan Oberman	(702) 555-1212	—	✔		Send resume & letter; will interview by phone @ 2nd cut

FIGURE 6.1   Sample Job Announcement Checklist.

Side Box 6.1

What Is This Nonprofit Organization Like?

You can learn a lot about nonprofit employers by looking them up online with Charity Navigator (2018) or Guidestar (2018). This is especially helpful when you are applying for work out of your local area and are not familiar with the employer's practices. Both sites provide data-based summaries of nonprofit entities, with an emphasis on finances. While they are intended for people who are considering making a donation, they are also very useful for job applicants who want to learn about the organization's infrastructure, spending, mission, and other features.

---

true not only at your sites, but in the classroom and around campus. Your first and best self-promotion is to aim to act with integrity, kindness, and the spirit of human services. You already participate in a human services community where others see your willingness to help others, attention to appropriate interpersonal interactions, and ways of managing inevitable disappointments and frustrations. These are the people who may draw your attention to a job, ask you to join their research team, write a reference letter, or put in a good word for you at an agency. Don't forget that you may be helping them out in these ways as well. Use your time as a student to build the skills of presenting yourself as a professional.

Some people find it easiest to start by writing about themselves. Try making a bullet list of your professional strengths and areas of proficiency. If this is hard, ask someone who knows you to help you out. This list can be the basis for parts of your resume or CV, characteristics you want your reference letter writers to include, and a cheat sheet for role playing job interviews. You can also ask a career counselor to help you translate your career and interest testing results into a self-description. For example, if you took the Big Five Personality Test and scored high on "openness" and "conscientiousness," reading the description of those factors can give you ready-made, non-jargon-y language to describe yourself. You might say something like, "One of my strengths is my curiosity. I've been told I'm a pretty creative problem solver. This relates to another one of my strengths. I work hard to come up with some solutions to try even if the situation is complex." You can illustrate these traits with an example from one of your human services experiences.

Trainings and Conferences

Another place to promote yourself and make connections with other professionals is at human services trainings and conferences. This could be an in-house training at your field site, a guest speaker at your college, a professional development seminar at another agency or offered as continuing education, or a regional or national conference. Any in-person professional gathering is an opportunity for professionals to get to know you. Events that provide meals or times to network can be especially effective. You probably will need to take the initiative—if a nametag identifying you as a student is available, wear it. Introduce yourself and ask people questions about the kind of work they do. You might ask them how they got started or whether they have advice for new graduates.

Some organizations offer student-focused trainings or schedule times for student conversations. Attend these and notice how other students express themselves. Some conferences invite student-faculty workshops and presentations. Even if you don't feel ready to present on your own, you may want to express your interest to a faculty member or supervisor whose work interests you. Presenting at a conference helps you connect with others in your field *and* gives you a resume or CV entry as described below.

If you are able to help submit a presentation proposal, ask if your program has scholarships or if your faculty member has grant funding to help with any conference expenses. You can also check with the conference organizer to learn whether student scholarships or discounts for students who volunteer at the conference are available. The National Organization for Human Services (NOHS) offers students conference registration at a reduced rate. It currently considers faculty-student presentation proposals. For more information, go to https://www.nationalhumanservices.org/ (NOHS, n.d.) and click the Conferences tab.

When you attend a training, professional development workshop, or conference, save the program or flyer and write down any specific information, such as the presenters' qualifications and the titles of specific talks. You may want to include a list of "Trainings and Conferences Attended" in your CV, or create a separate document to include with job applications. Save or scan these materials to create a record for yourself, since they are evidence of your continuing education, professional development, and coursework beyond your degree. This may help qualify you for a job, or, if a legal question ever arises, help demonstrate that you received training in the area that may be under scrutiny.

Membership in Professional Organizations

If attending a training or conference isn't economically feasible right now, look at joining a professional organization. This can be general, such as Rotary, or specific to human services.

Again, NOHS offers reduced student membership rates. Membership may give you access to scholarships or opportunities to write for an organization's newsletter. Professional organizations sometimes require you to agree to follow their ethical standards or code of conduct. Becoming a member of a professional organization shows an employer that you have a professional identity in the field and demonstrates your readiness to be held to professional standards. You should include your student memberships on your resume or CV.

Posting Your Credentials Online

Some students and professionals post their professional materials and credentials on online sites such as LinkedIn (https://www.linkedin.com) (2018) and Monster (https://www.monster.com) (2018). These and similar sites have tools that may be useful to you, and they increase your visibility. Explore them, read online reviews, and ask other people in human services which sites, if any, they have found to be useful.

If you are thinking about posting your materials online, remember the saying that *the Internet is not a series of closed rooms.* Here are several considerations and actions you will need to take for your privacy, safety, and professional presentation:

+ Most importantly, bear in mind that anything you post online is potentially accessible and public, even if it appears to be protected by a site. This means that your home address, phone number, email address, resume or CV, and goals or values statements may be available to anyone who searches for information about you. This could include past and future clients. The amount and quality of information available could also make it possible for someone to pretend they know you, or even to steal your identity. Think carefully about the information you make available on job sites. You may want to remove some of your data, like your home address, for this version of your materials.
+ Strongly consider using a separate, professional-only email address. You may also want to add a separate professional phone number, or code your personal contacts with a specific ring tone so that you will know that an unidentified caller may be an agency calling, or someone who has skimmed your number from the web. If feasible, you may want to rent a post office box for your professional correspondence. Do not post a photo with your resume on these sites.
+ Before you post anything professional online, search for your name(s) and images of yourself on several search engines. You can't do anything about the mug shot

of someone with the same name, but you can alert a potential employer that you are not that person. You may find that a great deal of your personal information, including tagged photos, is easily available. To the extent that you can, lock down or delete that information. If you need help, search for "lock down [Facebook, Pinterest, Yahoo!, etc.]." Your Facebook profile picture and cover photo are always public, so choose them wisely. Continue to use good "online hygiene" throughout your professional career.

+ Some job sites encourage you to allow the site to access your contacts or phone list. If you do so, everyone in your contacts may receive constant spam "invitations" from the site. This creates ill-will and raises questions about your ability to manage data. Don't allow sites to ruin your reputation.

+ Typos look bad no matter where they occur, but online misspellings and formatting problems may lead a casual reader to move to the next person's resume. When possible, post PDFs rather than word processed documents in order to retain your formatting.

+ If you post materials online, don't forget to update them every time you update your master copy.

Preparing Your Materials

To apply for jobs, you'll need an up-to-date, attractive resume or curriculum vitae (CV). You'll also want to put together a basic cover letter that you can adjust for each position.

Resume and Curriculum Vitae (CV, or Vita) Options

The terms *resume* and *CV* are sometimes used interchangeably. For our purposes, a resume is a brief or abbreviated report of your education, professional qualifications such as current licenses and certificates, previous jobs, and transferrable skills. A CV is a more extensive and detailed document. It includes the information in the resume, plus detailed descriptions of your previous work and other professional information. A resume may be as short as one page (although see more on this below), while a CV may be five, 20, or even more pages depending on your professional history.

It is important to provide your professional materials to a potential employer in the form they request. If the announcement asks for a CV, don't send a resume. If It asks for you to handwrite the information into an application form, don't write "see CV" on the form—fill it out. If you aren't sure, call or email to ask.

Resume and CV Templates

It is easy to find resume and CV templates to which you can add your information. For example, Microsoft Office has several templates in Word. Your career center or your community college's career center may have resume software available, as may your local or state employment office. Some temporary agencies also provide resume tools for their employees. Of course, you can make your own document, but this risks having inconsistent formatting.

In general, look for a template that is simple, uncluttered, and visually appealing. It should look professional and use at most two different typefaces. Resist the temptation to add graphics, and think about how your resume or CV will look when it is printed. For example, colored text or design elements look bad when they are printed in black ink.

Save your work frequently. When you think you have finished your document, save it, run a spelling and grammar check, then print it out and have someone with a good eye for detail read it for consistency and to check your formatting. Make your corrections, save a master file, then save or print it as a PDF. This ensures that your formatting remains as you intended it even if someone uses a printer or software with settings different from yours.

If you are submitting any materials electronically, look at each document's properties in your word processing program. Edit or remove information that may not be relevant to that application. For example, if you are using someone else's computer, you will want to remove their name from the author field. If you are applying for a job at the Boys and Girls Club, then using the same master document or editing the document to apply for Relief Nursery, be sure the document properties are edited as well and no longer say "B & G Club" or whatever heading you have provided.

Resumes

As noted, a resume typically is a short document characterizing your most relevant experiences and skills. It may include other information, such as a list of your professional references. However, consider whether to include extra information in the resume, or whether you can provide that information in your cover letter, on a form provided by the employer, or in an interview. A resume typically includes one line identifying each previous job or placement, and sometimes a sentence or bullet point identifying your major responsibilities in the position. It may also list transferrable skills—that is, your skills and training that can easily be used in another job role. The competencies and skills listed for your classes and site placements is a great place to start. Remember that prospective employers don't know the specifics of your program and that you need to demonstrate that you are the best applicant. You may want to identify your key courses related to the job ("Helping Skills," "Group Dynamics," "Working with Diverse Clients," "Case Management," etc.) and list them, refer to them in your cover letter, or choose the most important competencies associated with them to highlight under a "skills" heading. For example, if you apply for a job as an intake worker in a medical practice, note competencies from your classes such as "Training in active listening and motivational interviewing skills."

Utility of the Resume

A resume provides the employer with a quick look at your highlights, so it is important to think strategically and use your limited space wisely. For example, imagine you are applying for a job as a kindergarten one-on-one classroom aide. Your two previous practica, two previous jobs, and degree all clearly help qualify you for this position, and your cover letter and the job posting both identify the job as "One-on-one classroom aide, kindergarten." In this situation, there is no need to include a line on your resume that states, "Objective: Work as a one-on-one aide in early childhood setting." In general, including an objective is unnecessary and uses up your valuable space on the page. If your objective is as specific as the one in this example, it is obvious. If your objective is vague or general, it does not enhance your application and also wastes your space. For example, "Objective: A satisfying career providing quality human services" does not convey useful information and may suggest that you are not sure what you want to do.

Resume Tips

You may be told that a resume should be no more than one page long. Unless an employer has stated this requirement, it is not accurate for most human services positions. Try writing your resume without worrying about length. If it is more than two to three pages, consider using this extended master version as a source document from which you can create shorter resumes targeted to specific positions. For example, a person who has had a previous teaching career and is now re-specializing in human services might have a number of jobs listed on his master resume. When he applies for a human services classroom aide position, his previous teaching experiences are relevant and should be included, so his resume may be longer than one page. If he applies for a human services job that is not in an academic setting but involves working with children, he may want to list his educational positions, or note on his CV that he has "8 years' classroom experience as a K–5 classroom instructor (specific information available upon request)." He may also use this summary entry if he applies to a human services job that does not involve working with young children.

If you find that you cannot fit your relevant information into a resume format, you may want to consider listing only the last 10 years or only selected previous employment. Be sure that you indicate on the resume that it presents selected information only and that a complete list is available on request. You can prepare to apply for a variety of positions by creating a master resume, a one-page version, and a short version for each type of job role if you have more than one professional focus.

CVs

If you have a lot of relevant experience, you may find that a CV (also called a *vita*) is more effective. You can think of your CV as an annotated resume. It is more extensive and goes into more depth. It may include additional information, such as relevant awards you have received, professional memberships, and professional volunteer activities. CVs are more frequently requested in educational settings and for administrative or managerial positions. This reflects the understanding that these positions require more extensive experience. CVs are often requested for academic jobs. You may be able to look at your instructors' CVs on your college or program website, or by asking if you can review them.

Resume vs. CV

The biggest difference between a resume and a CV is the amount of information you provide about each previous placement and position. In human services, you may have

Resume vs. CV Style

Many parts of a resume and CV will look similar. However, a CV usually includes more information about your previous placements and jobs. Compare these examples:

Resume

9/16–6/17   **Resident Assistant**. Enid City College, West Enid, Oklahoma.

CV

9/16–6/17   **Resident Assistant**. Enid City College, West Enid, Oklahoma. 20 hours/week plus rotating emergency call. Primary supervisor: Marco di Palma, EdM, Resident Director.

Supervised all residential activities for 45 international students in a large on-campus residence hall. Developed orientation activities with staff, provided 5 or more hours of educational programming targeted to international students' needs per month. Monitored residents' physical and mental well-being, assessed building security. Received training in crisis response and engaged in crisis management. Students ranged from 18–27 years old, represented 21 countries, and spoke 14 languages in addition to English. Received a commendation from the Dean of Residence Life for outstanding performance during a substance abuse-related medical emergency.

performed a large number of job roles and responsibilities that are not evident from the job title. You may have had several supervisors whose degrees or certifications help you to meet a qualification (for example, you may be applying to a position that requires previous supervision by a certified drug counselor or a licensed social worker). The CV format gives you room for more extensive descriptions of not only your roles but your client populations. It may be very important for a potential employer to know not just that you co-led a cognitive-behavioral life skills group, but also that group members included older, Spanish-speaking Latinx clients and younger Latinx clients with disabilities.

Save a Master Copy!

Save a copy of your master resume as "master CV." This will be your most inclusive document. Include supervisors' names, degrees, and relevant certifications. Include exact dates, number of hours (per week or total), client characteristics, interventions used, and skills used. Add any information you could not fit in your resume. If you have a good GPA, you may want to include it. Don't forget about publications (your published letter to the editor about child abuse counts!); major projects completed during your education or employment; awards and honors (including those such as National Merit semifinalist, TUA human services honors society, and scholarships); voluntarism; and membership or leadership in your professional organizations, Rotary, Soroptimists, nonprofit boards, and other service activities. If you participated in a spring break service-learning trip to provide literacy education in a nearby city or helped on a medical mission to another country with your parents, include it. If you and your classmates raised $800, or procured 500 pairs of new socks for an AIDS service organization, list it! Keep this master CV updated to use as your source document for building specific resumes and CVs.

Tips for Resume and CV Writing

Track Everything!

If you don't do so already, start tracking everything now. Even if you're not ready to put it into a master resume or CV, you will be more accurate and save time if you keep a list of your professional activities and update it frequently.

Your Email Address

Use a professional email address. It is best to use your school account (if it will remain accessible to you), an account associated with your current job, or a personal account set up for this purpose. The account name should be professional as well. Use *MarissaGarcia*, not *pookieluvs2dance*. This may seem obvious, yet you might be surprised how many job applicants forget that an informal email address may predispose an employer against them. If you use a personal address from Gmail, Hotmail, Yahoo, or another large vendor, call a few days after sending your materials if you do not receive an acknowledgement. Because of spam and malware attacks, some employers' IT departments may periodically refuse email from these accounts.

Format and Describe Consistently

When you create your resume or CV, be sure your format and ways of describing your experience are consistent. Use active rather than passive statements, and present information in the same order for each job you describe (e.g., dates of employment or training, then the job title, then the agency, then your supervisor's information). Use the same format for any presentations you've made, trainings you've offered or assisted with, and publications. Common styles used in human services include APA, MLA, and Chicago style. If you are not sure which format to use, see if your campus offers writing assistance and can help you describe your activities in a professional style. You can also search for help pages on these styles online.

Print a copy of your documents to check the header and footer typeface and size, and to ensure that there is no extraneous or incorrect information included in these fields but not visible in an electronic copy.

Inconsistent and Consistent Presentation Listing Styles

Here is a list of presentations from a fictional student's resume. See if you can standardize the style and format so that this list is internally consistent. You can also try to put the list in APA, MLA, or Chicago style. What additional information do you need? What unnecessary information should be omitted? Can you help the student to express herself consistently and with standardized formatting?

- I am not my diabetes! How to listen to our clients. Fairfax Vir., practicum students and staff weekly meeting, Jan., 2019. Supervisor Gerald Wing. MS.
- Nian Zhen Jiang. 2018). Diabetes: A Problem For Rural Chinese Communities. Fairfax VA, senior project presentations, Fairleigh Hall, rm. 203. March 22nd.
- University of Fairfax, Workshop by Jiang, Nian Zhen 2019, Learn about diabetes Prevention in your Dorm!
- Jiang, "Nina." 5 tips for understanding diabetes. 2016, (poster presented), Scanlon community college, Fairfax, Virginia, in the Human Services honors program research talk.

Tailor Your Resume or CV to the Job Announcement

It is important to make sure that your resume or CV is complete within the requirements of the position. Some want you to list every job you've held, while others want only related experiences. If you have periods when you were not employed or were not in school, be prepared to explain them briefly in your cover letter (as described below).

It is helpful to read the job description carefully. The best way to be sure that you have answered all of the questions is to turn the application description into a set of points to address. For example, if the announcement states that applicants "must have at least 6 months' experience working with elders," you can make a note to yourself: "Describe 12 months' experience with elders at Goodman Center."

Use the Announcement's Terminology

Don't be afraid to use the job announcement's language in your application. Although you may be tempted to rephrase, this may work to your disadvantage. Some employers use a checkbox rating form that looks for the exact language used in applications, and using different language or not repeating the criterion can result in a lower score. For example, a job with the county sheriff's office might require "training in the use of DSM-5 for diagnostic purposes." Even if your transcript shows an Abnormal Psychology class, you may still receive no points if you indicate that you were "trained in developing diagnostic impressions." The best strategy is to use the posting's language and say something like "trained in developing diagnostic impressions using DSM-5." Although including this may seem repetitive, it is worth your effort to be explicit and demonstrate that your experience maps well onto the job requirements.

Protect Client Confidentiality in Descriptions of Previous Work

Many human services students have at least one previous job that was contracted directly with a family. This may have been something like providing after-school care and tutoring for a child with autism spectrum disorder, or helping a person with a disability with household chores. Think about how to characterize this job in a way that does not violate privacy or confidentiality. Consider the difference between these two ways of describing a job:

- Babysitter for the Lockwood family, 4334 W. Ardmore Terrace, Springfield, Pennsylvania: Babysat 12-year-old twins Maddie and Junie, picked them up at Springfield Friends Day School and took them to youth soccer practice. Made healthy snacks. Junie has HIV and sometimes needs help with her homework because she is tired.
- Family assistant, Springfield, Pennsylvania: Escorted two children, one with medically-related fatigue, to after-school activities; monitored and reinforced homework; and other household responsibilities.

Be Accurate and Honest

The information in your resume or CV should be true and accurate for both legal and ethical reasons. Misrepresenting your degree, degree status (e.g., listing your degree when you have not yet graduated), or license or certificate status can all be grounds for legal or ethical action, as can failing to disclose convictions when this is required, or omitting or falsifying information about why you left a previous position. You should include an explanation for anything that raises questions in your cover letter.

You may find that you do not meet a requirement listed for a particular job, but you may believe that you are a good candidate because you have transferrable skills. In this situation, describe your skills and explain why the employer should consider you for the position. Do not report or suggest that you have experiences that you don't. For example, if an announcement asks for "intervention experience working with elders" and you have provided intervention for people who are 40–50 years old in one setting and nonintervention services with people over 60 in your library volunteer role, describe this and explain how you believe this qualifies you.

Other Uses for Your CV

A current, detailed, and accurate master CV is also a very helpful tool if you want to apply for a license, certificate, other professional credential, or additional training programs.

It will speed the process and ensure that you do not unintentionally misrepresent yourself or leave out anything important.

Cover Letters

Think of your cover letter as a preview or teaser. If your job application were a television show and your cover letter were an ad, what should be included to make a reader want to see more? Your cover letter needs to provide the incentive for an employer to review the rest of your materials. For this reason, it should typically be short, to the point, and accurate, and it should include enough information about your qualifications and interests to stimulate a reviewer's interest.

Include a cover letter even if it is not requested, unless there is an instruction not to do so. This is your chance to entice an employer, so don't just write, "Thank you for reviewing my materials for Job Posting 123-45." Use the page to create a positive mental picture of yourself for the employer.

Don't Be Negative

Part of that positive picture comes through in how you discuss previous employers, agencies you have interacted with, and your academic team. If you had a negative experience and need to refer to it, use neutral language. It may be helpful to assume that the person reading your job application is the friend or family member of the person with whom you had a negative experience.

Keep Your Format Simple and Clean

Again, resist the temptation to use a lot of typefaces, colors, and graphics. Do not use exclamation points or colloquial or slang phrases, and do not use any emoticons. The look should be businesslike. A human services employer wants to know that you can communicate with clients, other professionals, insurance companies, other agencies, grant organizations, a licensing or certifying board, or the media in a way that presents the employer and organization as credible and professional.

Account for Gaps and Problem Areas

If your resume or CV shows periods when you were not employed or were not in school, you may want to address this in your cover letter. You may want to talk with your advisor or a career counselor about what to discuss and how to phrase it. A good rule of thumb is that if your application materials raise questions, your cover letter or interview should have a reasonable answer to them. Bear in mind that there are legal limits to what an employer can ask you.

Professional Wording for Self-Disclosures

Although your cover letter's tone should be professional, you may be asked to answer more personal questions. Again, it is helpful to go over any questions provided in the application announcement or forms and your responses with an advisor or career counselor. While you must answer honestly, you should consider what depth of response is appropriate for this particular application. For example, if the application materials ask why you are interested in a position as a group leader in a drug treatment center, you may or may not want to include your own or your family's experience with addiction. In this type of setting, personal experience with substance abuse may or may not be a mark in your favor. If you decide to make a self-disclosure, keep it short and in neutral language. Explain briefly how you have incorporated this personal experience into your professional goals or how it motivated you. An employer will want to know that your personal experience helps you to assist other people and that you understand that what worked for you may not work for someone else. Consider the different impressions made by these two statements:

- "My initial motivation for working in substance abuse treatment was the experiences of some family members. As I have sought out substance abuse training and placements, I have seen how effective 12-step interventions can be for many clients."
- "Sad to say, my mom was a drunk pretty much as long as I can remember! I had my moments, too, but let's just say AA saved my life. I am a firm believer that 12-step programs are the only way to go."

Promoting Yourself in Your Cover Letter

Don't be afraid to describe why you are a good match for the position, and don't hesitate to explain how you are a good match for a position for which you don't quite meet the listed qualifications. If you find it difficult to toot your own horn, ask your peers and faculty how they see you and what you should include in your letter. You can phrase it as, "It is difficult for me to promote myself, but my instructors say...."

Describe What the Job Offers You

Include the other side of the equation as well. What does this job provide that would be good for your professional growth? For example, you might say, "I am especially attracted by the opportunity to work with adjudicated adolescents. I have worked with teens and completed a class on adolescent criminality, and look forward to learning what works in the field."

Resources for Preparing Your Resume/CV and Cover Letter

The Internet and your career center offer a wealth of information and models or templates for putting together your written materials. What matters is that your products look professional. It is also useful to be able to edit and update your documents, which may argue for using your home word processing software or online templates that can be downloaded.

Here are just a few websites to get you started:

+ Hloom: https://www.hloom.com/ (2018)
+ CV to Resume Conversion Guide: https://ocs.yale.edu/sites/default/files/files/CV%20to%20ResumeWorkshopfinal.pdf (Yale University Office of Career Strategy, n.d.)
+ Workbloom Human Services Resume [actually a CV, but still very helpful to review]: https://workbloom.com/resume/sample/human-services.aspx (2006–2018)

Remember that different professions may prefer different styles and formats. If possible, ask your academic advisor, career counselor, and graduated peers to see successful examples. Your faculty members' CVs may be available online at your institution or LinkedIn. You can see how they describe their applied experiences, education, grants, awards, presentations, and other information.

Additional Materials

Some positions require or allow you to submit additional materials. In general, this is a good idea. However, if you are asked to include a work sample or case write-up, you may need permission from your supervisor or the client. Always double-check work samples for identifying client information, since this is a breach of privacy or confidentiality. Note that you have changed or omitted information to protect client privacy; it is not sufficient just to remove or cross out the client's name. Specific information that may identify the client should also be removed. For example, if your work sample is a case management disposition for your client Ethan Rhys, a 22-year-old with a Welsh accent who works as a singing balloon-delivery clown, he will be easily identifiable even if you remove his name. You would need to alter other information that is identifying but irrelevant to his presenting issues and your report.

Your Professional Portfolio

During your academic program, you may have assembled an online or hard copy work portfolio. Items commonly included in human services portfolios are a general cover letter, academic transcripts, field placement or work evaluations, letters thanking you or identifying your role in a human services-related activity, news articles about your human services projects or those in which you have participated, work samples, abstracts of projects such as your senior capstone project, professional memberships and certificates, lists of continuing education completed, and similar. You may also have some standing reference letters. If you have not collected these materials and others that demonstrate your engagement in the field, consider doing so.

When you apply for a job, think about whether it is appropriate and helpful to include copies of materials from your portfolio. Don't include the whole portfolio, because this creates extra work for the evaluator. In addition, some of the materials may be irrelevant to the job or even work against you.

Use New Rather Than Standing Reference Letters

Some positions will request reference contact information and some will ask for letters. Generally, do not send standing reference letters from your portfolio. Instead, ask the writers (or more current writers) if they would provide a new letter that is specific to the job. A standing letter can shed a negative light on your application if the evaluator wonders why you are submitting an old letter rather than a new one. They may wonder if your writer is unwilling to provide a new letter, or if no current supervisor will write one, or even if you are trying to disguise legal or ethical problems that have arisen since the old letter was written. Your writer may not have realized you would be using their letter for applications, and you do not want to alienate that person!

If you have a good reason to use a letter from your portfolio, ask the writer, if possible, for permission to use it for this purpose. Perhaps the letter is relatively recent, or articulates specific, relevant activities you engaged in at that placement, or includes specific praise for your talents. Perhaps that writer is no longer available or the agency no longer exists. In your cover letter, explain why you are including this standing reference letter or any material from your portfolio.

Sending Your Application

Before you seal the envelope, go back to the application or your checklist for that position. Have you included all the materials requested? Have you added a cover letter or optional materials? Have you double-checked all documents for inaccurate or unnecessary information in headers, footers, and properties? Have you double-checked for client confidentiality, including checking the document's headers, footers, and properties?

In addition, if you are emailing materials, check your email signature line and any other information that is hidden from your view. Is it up to date and accurate? Is it spelled correctly? Does it include a quote that may not be appropriate for a professional communication? This may not be the time to declare your love for Ariana Grande in your signature line.

Interviews

Some of your applications will result in an invitation to interview. The more prepared you are and the more you have practiced interviewing, the more relaxed and competent you will be. You may have great written materials, but your self-presentation, interpersonal skills, and engagement in the interview will be evaluated as well, especially in this field. Don't forget about your professional interpersonal training! It is just as relevant in a job interview as it is when you interview a client. Remember that the Microskills Basic Listening Sequence (Ivey, Ivey, & Zalaquett, 2018) can help you build and maintain rapport with your interviewer.

Before You Get the Call

Telephone and Voice Mail Considerations

You want to make a good first impression, so pay attention to details that demonstrate your professionalism. You have already used a professional email address and checked your signature line. Now make sure that the phone number you have provided has a professional voicemail recording. "You have reached Marissa Habib. Please leave a message and your number, and I'll get back to you as soon as I can" is perfectly acceptable. Cats meowing "Jingle Bells" or a message from your 3-year-old are not.

If you have had a drink, are corralling twin toddlers, are in the shower, or are in the middle of rewiring an electrical socket, don't answer the phone at the number you provided in your application unless you recognize that the caller is not from the job site. It is better to call back in a few minutes when you are prepared, unfrazzled, and not up on a ladder with live wires in your hand. Similarly, if the number you gave is for a shared phone, alert the other people who might answer that you have job applications out and need them to answer calls politely and professionally.

Online Considerations

Do an online search for your name. Some prospective employers will look at your online presence. If you use LinkedIn or similar services, make sure your information is current. You may need to make your privacy settings more restrictive, or attempt to remove or hide some information or photos. Don't forget to check your Twitter feed. Remember that your Facebook profile and cover photos are always public, so be sure they don't show you in a bathing suit, with a daiquiri, or showing off your new tattoo. Remember, if an employer can find it, so can your clients.

Preparing for the Interview

There are many ways to prepare for interviews. Some activities that include practice interviews appear later in this chapter.

Review Your Materials

The first and easiest way to prepare is to review the materials you submitted so that they are fresh in your mind. Next, start a file for each job. Review the job posting and make some notes about key points. Remember to use the announcement's language. Look up the site online and take notes, and talk with classmates or faculty and staff who have insights about this agency. Add the key points to your notes.

Write Questions

For any position, you will have general questions that you might ask about any job. These may include questions about a typical weekly or daily schedule, whether hours are set or vary, how many night or on-call shifts are included, and similar logistical questions. Although you may need to ask what the job pays or have questions about the benefits or vacation, it is best not to lead with these. Instead, list them separately and consider asking them later in an interview or when you receive an offer.

You will also have specific questions about this position. It is important for you to develop several specific questions that show you have done your research about the site. For example, you may want to ask, "I see that you have a weekly all-staff meeting. Is this when client progress is discussed, or is there a separate clinical meeting?" Or, "I see that your social workers lead psychoeducational parent training groups. I'm very interested in parent training. Would I be able to observe or help in one of these groups?" Make sure that your questions aren't answered on the agency's website.

Notes

You may want to develop a list of three key bullet points about yourself, and three about the site. You can put the list at the top of the list of questions you have for the site as a reminder of what you want to emphasize. Leave space in your list so you can take notes on their answers, especially if you are applying for several jobs. You can write your notes immediately after the interview.

Professional Attire

Have a professional-looking interview outfit that you are comfortable wearing. What "professional" means will vary by region, agency, and even job role. However, it is better to arrive dressed a little too formally rather than not formally enough. Even if you know that the position requires helping to clean up homeless camps and employees wear boots, jeans, and dirty t-shirts to work, you should still wear interview clothing that is appropriate to an office job.

Some students choose a day each week to wear professional attire to classes. You want to know before you're interviewing that your jacket is a dog fur magnet. Some programs, schools, or communities have a free interview clothes closet or exchange. Ask your advisor or other students, and if there is nothing like this, consider starting one!

The Interview

Organizing Yourself

Set out your materials, such as your list of questions, a pen, your reading glasses, your car keys, a lint roller, and anything else you'll need for the interview the night before. Make sure your interview clothing is clean and ready to go. Map your route if you are not sure how to get to the interview.

Plan to arrive early, especially if you are not familiar with the area or anticipate traffic. You want to arrive feeling calm, with time to use a restroom, drink a little water, and find the waiting area. If offered coffee, you may want to consider whether you will spill it on yourself, or what you will do with the cup when someone wants to shake your hand and you are holding your notepad in one hand and the coffee in the other.

Interview Questions

Interviewers may or may not tell you how long the interview is and how many questions they will ask. Consider each question, answer it briefly but specifically, and then determine whether you have answered all of the parts of the question or ask, "Have I answered your question or would you like me to go into more depth?" Keep track of your time! This is a skill that you can build in your practice interviews with peers.

The questions you will be asked will vary, but it is likely that you will be asked at least some of these questions:

+ Tell us a little about yourself. What do you do for fun [or a similar question intended to put you at ease]?
+ What interests you about this position?
+ What are your qualifications for this position?
+ What are you like as a member of a work team?
+ What are your areas of strength and weakness in relation to this position?
+ What sets you apart from other applicants?
+ Describe a time when you encountered an ethical challenge in a professional setting. What happened, and what did you do?
+ Describe a time when you had a conflict with a coworker. What happened, and what did you do?
+ Here is a [job-related, clinical, or ethics] scenario. What would you do in this situation?
+ What do you see as the diversity considerations in this scenario?

You can find other human services interview questions by searching online (e.g., at Glassdoor, https://www.glassdoor.com/Interview/human-services-specialist-interview-questions-SRCH_KO0,25.htm, 2018), asking your peers, and asking your faculty and staff. Your career center and field placement coordinator may also have lists of common interview questions.

Every Aspect of Your Interaction With the Site Is Part of Your Interview

Interviewees are usually nervous, and most interviewers will attempt to help you relax. However, even if the interviewer seems friendly and warm, remember that this is still an interview and that what you say is being evaluated. (In fact, remember that everyone at the site, including the receptionist and currently placed students, may be asked for input on how you interacted with them.) Practice interviews can help you feel confident and relaxed while still retaining your poise and professional demeanor.

Be Respectful of Personnel, Agencies, and Clientele

Consider the different feelings evoked by these statements. If you were interviewing someone, how would each statement affect your hiring decision?

- Anyways, that just proved that job and that manager was not for me! I got out of there as soon as I could!

- My supervisor and I saw the situation differently. After we discussed it, I did what she asked, but I still had concerns I needed to follow up on.

- My supervisor was pretty dumb. I could have run the place better myself.

- Of course, I've never come to work high!

- I liked some of the clients, but a lot of them were really creepy.

- It's hard for a school to meet everyone's needs when there are big budget cuts. Morale generally went down and there wasn't a lot we could do. After a while, I didn't feel like I could do my job effectively.

- Then I got all the other interns together and we sent a petition to the executive board.

- It was a challenging client group, and I really had to explore my own values and assumptions. It took some time and my manager seemed impatient with me.

- They wouldn't give me my religious holidays off. That's illegal!

- My evaluations were good and I like the work, but I'm ready to move on to a more challenging position.

How could you express the important information in the less-professional statements more appropriately?

Stay Positive

As with your cover letter, it can be easy to slide into negative statements about previous supervisors, sites, and clients, but resist the temptation. Remember, the interviewer is not collecting information about other agencies but is evaluating what you will be like as their employee. Your disrespectful comments about others raise the question, *What will he say about me, our agency, and our clients?*

Don't Forget to Ask Your Questions About the Position

Interviewers are likely to ask what questions you have for them. Be sure to ask some site-specific questions, such as "If I'm hired in the homeless youth day program, will I also be able to visit or work during the evening shift?" In addition, and especially if the ad was

200 Tests

Ivy, a new BSW, was delighted to accept a job at a community college in a nearby county. She would be working as a resource aide at the educational access office for students with disabilities. Based on the job announcement and her interview, she eagerly anticipated shifts welcoming and scheduling students at the front desk, meeting individually with students to connect them with campus and community partners, leading study session groups one evening a week, and proctoring tests for students with academic accommodations. She knew that several previous resource aides had been offered graduate school tuition stipends if they were successful at the work and interested in becoming counselors in the program.

In mid-October, she was offered the job and negotiated a start date of December 15 because at graduation she had made a 6-month commitment to her current employer, a retailer at the mall. The office agreed to this date, although they expressed eagerness for her to start, since the position was open at mid-year only because the previous aide had abruptly moved home to care for his mother.

Ivy found a great apartment near the college. The rent was a little high for her retail job, but her father loaned her the first and last month's rent since her salary would be higher once she started work. She moved in early November and commuted to her retail job.

On November 30, Ivy received a puzzling email from the educational access office coordinator asking Ivy to notify her immediately "when you have the tests graded." When Ivy expressed confusion, she learned that one of her job responsibilities was to grade the tests that she proctored. There was a backlog of tests administered by the previous aide. Ivy wrote back to say that she had not been aware of this responsibility and that her employment did not begin for several weeks. The office director called and left a message asking if she would please help out. "We'll give you comp time at Christmas—that will be nice for you—but this is one of the key responsibilities associated with this position. I know we talked about this at the interview! Jimmy leaving has really inconvenienced us, and someone has to grade those tests and get scores back to the instructors by December 8 at the latest, or they won't be able to get grades in on time. That would look terrible for the office and we'd probably lose the aide position in the next funding cycle. It shouldn't take you too long. There are only about 200 tests, and some of them are multiple choice."

- If you were Ivy, what would you wish you had done before accepting the position?
- What are Ivy's options now?
- How would you negotiate with the office director?

vague, check your understanding of the job responsibilities. You don't want to accept a job offer and then learn that you will be expected to engage in major activities you didn't know about and might not enjoy. Take notes on this conversation so that you can think about it at home and, if you accept the job, go over the tasks again so that everyone is on the same page. This can be useful about a month into a new job, when you may want to ask about activities that you have not yet begun or discuss activities you are asked to do that were not articulated at the interview.

After your interview, send a note or email to the lead interviewer or the designated employment contact person. In addition to thanking them for the interview, you may want to express your excitement about the position or provide brief additional information. Keep it short and professional.

Activities to Prepare Yourself for Your Job Search

In addition to the tips already discussed, here are more activities to prepare you for your application and interviews.

Construct Your Resume and CV

With several classmates, prepare your resumes and CVs.

+ If you already have one or both, update them. Give each other constructive feedback on your documents, looking for completeness, accuracy, consistent style, spelling, and clarity. Play with different formats to see what looks best to you and your friends.
+ Take your documents to a career counselor (or a professional who has offered to help you with this). Get their opinions and suggestions, too.

Before You Interview

With several friends, practice your interviewing skills. Use actual job announcements and information.

+ Provide the interviewers with a job announcement and your materials. The interviewers can generate questions or find questions online. Set up an interview room as realistically as possible (e.g., sign up for a conference room rather than using someone's living room). Interviewers and the interviewee should dress professionally. Interviewers should introduce themselves and may let the interviewee know how much time the interview will take or how many questions they will ask. They should ask some questions specific to the interviewee's written materials. After the interview, interviewers should provide positive feedback and constructive feedback. If possible, practice the actions suggested by the constructive feedback immediately. For example, if the feedback is "You have a nice smile, but you smiled all the way through, even when you were telling a story about horrific child abuse," the interviewee should try to answer the question with attention to his facial features. Take a break, then change roles until everyone has had a chance to practice. Plan to meet several times so that you become as comfortable as possible with being interviewed.

 * If it is relevant, you can also practice telephone and Skype or video conference interviews.

Reengage in Values Clarification

Refreshing yourself about your values and reasons for being in the field (see Chapter 1) will help you answer questions about the specific job and human services in general.

 * In writing or in a recorded conversation with a friend, see if you can describe your professional values. You can also explain your current and long-term professional goals. Do this several times until you have written or recorded some clear statements that you can practice saying and memorize.
 * Refresh your understanding of your professional ethics. Think of examples of times when you faced an ethical challenge or had to respond to someone's unethical behavior at school or in a job. Link these examples to ethical standards. Practice telling these stories in a way that protects people's privacy.

Stepping Stones vs. Your Dream Job

People take a job for different reasons. For one person, a job might be a stepping stone to a future, more desirable job. For another person, the same position might be their dream job. For another person, the job may have no appeal except the paycheck. Any of these might be fine for you, depending on the circumstances. Thinking about the goodness of fit may help you decide which jobs to apply for or whether to accept an offer.

Your first human services job, or first job after graduating, might be a rung in a ladder that provides the experience and competence that lets you climb up a step toward the kind of work you feel passionate about. Many people's first professional job is an entry-level position from which they hope to be promoted or that they plan to leave after some time. Sometimes this is a temporary position or one that will qualify you to apply for a job that requires more sophisticated skills.

Another person might land their perfect job and continue to find it satisfying for many years. They might even have only one professional job in most or all of their career. This may happen immediately or after they explore several other positions.

Yet another person may need to pay the bills. When it comes down to it, it may not matter, at least in the immediate present, what the job is. A temporary position or a job with a health insurance plan may be ideal for someone with immediate needs, or for someone who is new to an area, is having trouble finding other work, or wants to buy time to apply for other, more desirable work. It may not lead to a career and it may not be satisfying, but it allows the person to take care of business and consider other options.

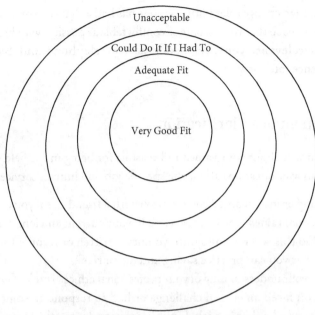

Unacceptable

Could Do It If I Had To

Adequate Fit

Very Good Fit

(After DiMarco, 1997 and personal communication)

FIGURE 6.2   Simplified On Target Model.

Of course, there are also jobs that a person simply won't consider. You may draw the line at a job that is not in human services, or that serves a population for which you have no affinity or training, or that doesn't pay well enough to cover your expenses, or where you just didn't feel good after an interview. It may not provide child care, or it may require you to live in another country for a year. Again, it is fine to determine that this job won't work for you, but remember that it may suit someone else's needs well, so think of it as *a bad fit* rather than *a bad job*.

In addition to career and interest tests, there are other ways to sort through potential jobs in order to clarify how good a fit each may be for you under your present circumstances. DiMarco's *Career Transitions: A Journey of Survival and Growth* (1997) is devoted to an in-depth exploration of work and career shifts. DiMarco provides detailed worksheets of her On Target model for thoroughly investigating eight dimensions to consider, such as skills and energy resources. We will consider only the three broad categories of "very good fit," "adequate fit," and "unacceptable fit" (pp. 1–9), adding an additional, practical category, which can be thought of as "I could do it if I had to" to characterize work that you would do if necessary for your safety and survival but which would not be acceptable in the longer term (DiMarco, personal communication) (see Figure 6.2).

You can use this simplified worksheet in several ways.

- Think about your previous jobs of field experiences. Write each one in the ring it belongs in. Have you had a job that was a very good fit for your interests, skills, and needs? Remember that either a dream job or a stepping stone job could fit in this category, depending on your situation at the time. What about jobs that were an adequate fit for you? These might be stepping stones or jobs that were good enough and met your needs. They might also be jobs that used to be a very good fit but changed (or you changed and the job no longer fit as well). Next, list jobs that you did because you had to. You may have needed the job to survive, but you would not want to do it any longer than necessary. Finally, have you had jobs that you would now consider unacceptable for any reason? You can use a bigger worksheet to position the jobs closer to or farther from the next ring, or you can overlap rings if some aspects of the job were perfect, for example, but others were only satisfactory.

- Once you have filled in your previous jobs, think or talk with a classmate about each job and explain why you located it where you did. You may also want to discuss where you would have placed the job when you first got it. Did your engagement with the job change over time? Do you notice any patterns that could help you identify jobs that are a better fit?

- Make a list of the positions to which you are currently applying or those you are considering. Describe the major characteristics, features, and undesirable aspects of each position as best you can. For example, you might write "K–2 Special Needs Classroom Assistant. Skills are a good match. Enjoy special needs kids. Prefer older kids. Would like supervising field trips. Don't like helping feed kids. Could transfer to higher grade later. Advancement requires teaching certificate. Good health benefits. Pay okay. People who work there like the supervisor. Have to work one night a month. 180 work days a year. Would need summer job." Add to your descriptions over a few hours or even a few days, as you think of other factors.

- Use a fresh copy of the worksheet to explore each job. Write in each characteristic of the job in the location that reflects the goodness of fit for you. Look at each job. Where do most of its features fall? Are you missing any information that is drawing you to or pushing you away from the job? When you compare the different jobs, which looks like the best fit and which looks like the worst for you?

- Using a fresh copy of the worksheet, place each of the jobs you applied for as best you can. How do they seem to compare? Are you uncertain where to place some? Can you get more information about a position to help you place it?

- Looking at all of your worksheets, can you identify any of your must-have characteristics? Are the jobs clumping in the "adequate" range? Try abstractly listing the things that make a job appealing for you. Are these represented in your worksheets? Would it help to look for work that has these aspects?

If the activities in this section interest and help you, you might enjoy going deeper into different aspects of your past, current, or potential jobs using DiMarco's (1997) workbook.

Licensure, Certification, and Similar Credentialing

If you want to increase your qualifications for a variety of jobs, or want to be eligible for promotion to a position that requires it, consider obtaining a license, certificate, or similar credential. Like membership in a professional organization, licensure and certification show that you are willing to hold yourself to higher professional ethical standards, as well as the legal standards that come with these credentials. Some credentials require supervised postdegree practice. Most, if not all, have application and renewal fees.

Associate's- and Bachelor's-Level Licensure and Certification

Many states do not have license or certificate requirements for professionals with associate's or bachelor's degrees. Talk with an advisor and look at local job announcements to learn more about your area's requirements and preferences. A criminal record may restrict your eligibility for some licenses, certificates, or other qualifications. If you have a record or are aware of other problems that may appear on a local or national background check, talk with the credentialing organization, or a faculty or staff person who is familiar with this issue.

Managing a Felony Conviction

Disclosing a felony or other required legal information that you did not report when you entered your program may lead to ethical or legal proceedings or an evaluation of your status in the program. This issue may arise when you engage in a background check, apply for a job, or need to fill out (or have faculty or supervisors fill out) a legal document or character attestation.

If you are able to consult anonymously or hypothetically about legal issues (ideally before applying), this may preserve your privacy. To receive accurate information, you need to consult an expert in the jurisdiction in which you will be applying.

A legal record will not necessarily preclude you from obtaining a credential. Be prepared to document and explain the circumstances and steps you have taken to prevent being in that situation again as part of the application process. If any part of your legal record can reasonably and feasibly be expunged, you may want to start this process early. Your college may have a legal consultant available for students or may be able to refer you to low-cost community services. Again, don't forget to consult your community's service help manual or website.

Licensing Requirements

Licenses are issued by individual states for professional work in that jurisdiction. Licensure requirements, including required coursework and supervised field work, vary by state and license type, as do the laws under which a licensee functions and the scope of practice allowed for different licenses. A license typically requires one or more tests, often including legal, ethical, and general professional knowledge questions. It also requires transcripts, documentation of your supervised practica and other field placements, and reference letters, as well as attestations about your ethical and legal conduct. You may hold licenses in multiple jurisdictions. Although many licenses associated with human services are for professionals with graduate degrees, you may be eligible for some licenses if your jurisdiction offers them in your human services specialty area. Your academic program can identify these for you. If you are interested in licensure in a different state or province, try contacting an undergraduate human services program in that jurisdiction.

Certification Requirements

While a license typically meets a state requirement in order for you to be allowed to practice, a certificate may or may not. Certificates that meet a jurisdictional requirement are similar to licenses. A big difference is that while some certificates meet a legal practice requirement for your jurisdiction, others simply serve as a credential that demonstrates that you have met the set of standards represented by taking a professional development training. For example, you may receive a certificate in motivational interviewing (MI) issued by the organization overseeing a training you completed successfully. This is a certification of your professional development activity and demonstrates that you now have more knowledge in this area. It may allow you to provide formal MI services. However, it is not the same thing as receiving a state-required, role, or professional status-related certification that is more like a license.

Most states require a state-level certification if you want to work as a substance abuse interventionist. Many human services students begin or even complete coursework and supervised hours for a substance abuse and chemical dependency certification while still enrolled in their programs. The requirements often can be met through academic or continuing education courses after graduation as well. This certification expands your scope of practice, allowing you to perform some interventions or assessments that would not be in your normal human services scope of practice. You may also have opportunities to obtain national certification, depending on the area of practice represented by the certifying organization. Take a look at NAADAC: The Association for Addiction Professionals (n.d.; see also Appendices G and H) to learn about national options and requirements.

Your professional organizations can provide you with information about whether your areas of specialization are associated with national certification options. One example of a national certification that is not required by states or provinces but which demonstrates your commitment to professional practice standards is the Center for Credentialing and Education's (CCE) Human Services–Board Certified Practitioner certificate (2016b; see also Appendices C and D). CCE offers additional certificates for which you also may be eligible.

The Qualified Mental Health Associate (QMHA) and Other Designations

Additional options, such as the Qualified Mental Health Associate (QMHA) and state-level designations such as "peer navigator" or "paraprofessional trainer," may be available to you as well. These titles typically are not a license or certificate that travels with you but rather a set of criteria that, if met by you and approved by the state, allow you to work in a job role for which this designation is a requirement. As an example, you might want to apply for a behavioral health support provider role that lists "QMHA-eligible" as a requirement or preference. You may meet the criteria and document this or follow the instructions for doing so in the announcement. Or you might be close to meeting the criteria and indicate this in your application. If you are offered the job, you and your employer will complete your application, and, if successful, you may be able to list your professional qualifications as "Lee Takahashi, BA, QMHA." When you leave this position, you may indicate on your resume that at this job you were a QMHA, but you will most likely need to be requalified at your next position. QMHA and QMHP (QMH Professional) requirements may even vary in different counties in the same state, so stay alert for possible differences.

Whether you obtain a license, certificate, or other qualification, you probably will have requirements related to supervision, continuing education, or professional development, and ethical standards or a code of conduct to follow. Be sure you are familiar with these requirements so that you do not miss deadlines.

Graduate School

Many resources are available for undergraduates who are exploring applying to graduate programs. While some students plan to do so, either immediately or eventually, others do not. They may be first-generation college students, or have financial or geographical constraints. They may have poor grades or low test scores, or simply think they "aren't graduate school material." They may want to work for a few years before considering an advanced degree. It's worth keeping the graduate school option in mind, even if it is just a possibility down the road. The materials you develop and maintain in your job search are identical or very similar to what you will need to apply to graduate school, so keep copies of your documents just in case you decide to apply.

Tips for Avoiding Common Job Application Errors and Problems

To give yourself your best chance to be seriously considered for a job, pay attention to these tips and suggestions:

- Double-check that you have included all requested materials and followed all instructions.
- Think of your application and interview as "first date" behavior. Remember that your communication with the site and interview are likely to be the only samples of your behavior that the interviewers actually experience directly. If your materials and interpersonal style are sloppy, disrespectful, or off-putting, why would an employer want another "date" with you?
- If you clearly are not qualified for a position, apply elsewhere. Applying for a job that requires an MSW and social worker license eligibility when you have a BS

in early child education will not get you a job, and may cause an evaluator to flag you as someone who does not read instructions.

+ Be specific. It is okay to reuse parts of your application or develop some standard answers to questions, but don't make everything boilerplate or general. You should have specific answers, comments, and questions for each site.

+ Use professional but straightforward language. Remember that the interviewer does not know your program's jargon or acronyms. Avoid slang and obscenities, but don't "talk on stilts."

  + Too informal: So y'know, I, like, like to ask each resident, "What's yer poison and how stoned have you been the last couple weeks?" LOL.

  + About right: When I interview the new residents, I ask, "What's your drinking and drugging been like in the last two weeks?"

  + Too formal: Upon admission and unit orientation, I preferentially inquire of each new program participant, "Which substances of abuse have you most characteristically imbibed or otherwise ingested, and in what quantity, during the course of the previous fortnight?"

+ To the extent that you can, demonstrate that there is a good fit between your training, skills, and interests, and the position. A good job is mutually beneficial to you and the agency.

What to Do If You Can't Get a Job

Despite a great deal of effort on your part, sometimes it is hard to find a job. This can be demoralizing and make it hard to keep applying. If you are a member of a minority group, have a disability, or are a first-generation student, you may wonder if discrimination is playing a role. No matter who you are, it can be challenging not to feel inadequate.

Here are a few suggestions for attuning your job search:

+ Are your written materials clear, accurate, well-formatted, spell-checked, grammatical, and engaging? Have you described yourself and your experience professionally and completely? Ask several trusted professionals to review your written materials. These might include your academic advisor, your faculty members, a career counselor, or even a writing tutor. It is sometimes surprising how difficult it is to review your own writing accurately.

+ Are you interviewing well? Again, ask others to help you evaluate your performance. This may include recording mock interviews and reviewing them.

+ Have you experienced legal or other problems that may be excluding you from consideration? If you cannot expunge your legal record, or if significant problems exist, consult with a career counselor in order to strategize about how you can best compensate for this.

+ Are you applying for too narrow a range of jobs? Jobs only in a small geographical area? Consider ways to expand your options, including using career testing to identify occupations and roles that are a good fit for you but which you may not have considered.

+ Are you qualified for the jobs? You may need to look at positions with different requirements, or seek more training, education, or credentials.

+ Are you being too picky? As in buying a house or committing to a relationship, apply the 80% rule: Ask yourself, "Does this job match my interests and needs at about 80% or higher? Will the unmet needs pose a problem?" Use the Bureau of Labor Statistics (2018a) and other resources from Chapter 1 to learn whether your salary expectations are accurate.

+ Have your reference letters raised issues or introduced a problem? Talk with your writers to see if they have any concerns that you could address or take care of. Explain that you are not getting interviews (or job offers) and ask if you could go over the letter with them.

+ If the economy is poor, few jobs are available, or no available human services jobs interest you, are you willing to consider a survival job that you could do for a limited time (DiMarco, 1997)?

Fortunately, many human services professions have openings and are projected to expand. Chapter 7 looks toward the future of human services.

Figure Credits

Fig. 6.2: Cara DiMarco, Career Transitions: A Journey of Survival and Growth. Copyright © 1997 by Prentice Hall PTR.

Chapter 7

Preparing for the Future of Human Services

Living in the Future

Congratulations! You went to sleep in the present last night, and today you have awakened in the future. The changes may be too small to notice, but if you look back a few years, they become more obvious. Changes in communities, cultures, economies, and technologies affect the field of human services, sometimes for better and sometimes for worse. To give just two examples, the National Child Traumatic Stress Network was established in 2001 (Clay, 2012), but the rate of uninsured people has climbed in the last two years (Williams, 2018). Changes may be anticipated or surprise you, but change is inevitable. One of your responsibilities as a human services professional is to keep up with change as best you can in order to provide the most informed and up-to-date care for your clients.

Consider these scenarios, 50 years apart:

- 1969: Ellen drives her old VW Beetle to her job at about 7:30 a.m. She needs to be there early to unlock the door. Three men and a woman are waiting outside, smoking cigarettes and talking. Ellen, who completed 3 years of a sociology degree before deciding the system was corrupt and that she didn't want to work in a hospital, founded this drop-in center so that homeless people who had been up all night would have a place to crash during the day. The two-room storefront is furnished with used chairs and sofas. Ellen's uncle pays the rent, which is low because the neighborhood is run down. He also comes up with a little salary for Ellen to supplement donations, which come mostly from tourists who visit the neighborhood to gawk at the hippies. About five to 25 people will hang out for much of the day at Ellen's place. It doesn't have a name yet, but the Rolling Stones' new album has a song called "Gimmie Shelter" and Ellen recently decided this would be a good name. She thinks that if somebody would donate a cassette tape recorder, she could record the album at home on a quiet night and bring

121

it in to play for the clients. There is no phone at Ellen's place, and there are no working phones nearby. Ellen sometimes gets the conversation going, and there have been some good rap sessions. Ernesto sometimes comes over with people who are having a bad trip or are freaking out. Ellen keeps an eye on them and makes sure they stay hydrated. Sometimes Ernesto gives a little talk on what to do if your friend overdoses. Ellen isn't sure what Ernesto does the rest of the time, but she thinks he's a male nurse.

+ 2019: Ellen, 71 years old and still going strong, pings a ride service from her phone because her Prius is in the shop. Her PayPal account is charged automatically and she is dropped at the Equinox Recovery Center, where she reminds a couple of clients that they need to be farther from the door if they're going to vape. She is just in time to lead her morning drop-in Meditation for Addiction Recovery group, so she plays the opening instructions from YouTube to the Bluetooth speaker. The receptionist lets her know that one of her usual clients messaged on the agency portal to say he would be a little late for his family therapy session at 2:00 o'clock because his daughter's wife had to debug the bank's mainframe. She also tells Ellen that they have to break out some time to go over the accounts because somebody has been entering incorrect CPT codes again, and she's worried some of the clients' insurance carriers won't pay for their methadone. She also mentions that the rent is going up another $750 a month, and Ellen may need to push Ernesto to write another grant to cover it. Ellen reminds her that Ernesto is visiting his grandson in Chile, so she should text him at his personal number to see if he can do it or if he wants to bring in some of the graduate students from the grant writing class he teaches online. Ellen sometimes misses the face-to-face time with some of her clients, but she has to admit that the new apps SAMHSA trained her on are great for behavioral reinforcement. After her group, Ellen enters client notes in the agency's database, and for a few of the clients, in the parole and probation database so their parole officers can read them; Facetimes with the accountant at the downtown location; checks her personal Google Calendar for conflicts; then blocks out a time with the receptionist on Outlook. She sets a phone alarm to remind her to submit her continuing education documentation and pay her certificate renewal, then checks her email. The background checks for the new interns should be showing up soon, and she wants to talk with Susan about whether she's far enough along in her recovery to co-lead the cognitive therapy workshop. And she needs someone credible to give a talk on ways marijuana can still be a problem even though it's legal. Her phone beeps the time and she realizes that if she walks over to the hospital, she has just enough time to have someone figure out why her insulin pump won't synch data with the doctor's office, and the walk will get her up to 5000 steps for the day.

Many human services agencies have evolved from small, peer-run efforts to provide services that were not available in the conventional medical and social systems of the late 1960s and the 1970s. Some have prospered, growing into established community resources. Others have closed or been absorbed by other organizations. Ellen's grassroots storefront has become a thriving multisite chemical dependency and recovery agency, with all the benefits and headaches that come with change.

The Impact of Technology

Technological advances play a major role in the progression of the human services field, especially if the vast medical field is included. As only one example, Ellen's first shop could have had a landline with a dial. Today, most of the staff and clients have phones, the majority of which function as computers. The way the business is organized, managed, documented, and paid for has changed with technology, as have the many options for contacting, providing services to, and billing for clients. In 1969, Ellen's records, if she kept them, might have been handwritten on a legal pad and kept in a file cabinet or desk drawer. Today, Ellen hopes her cloud access doesn't fail, and that she remembers the password for her encrypted USB drive. Ellen's business is highly networked in a worldwide constellation of other providers, organizations, governmental agencies, insurance companies, and data storage. She can access millions of studies, articles, data sets, manuals, best practices documents, blogs, book reviews, and more.

Ellen has to keep up with technology in order to remain a competent human services professional. Like you, she learns about new hardware and software from her friends and colleagues, and absorbs some of her skills automatically from online sources, ads for new products, and alerts from her professional organizations. She recently attended a half-day workshop on current telehealth technologies and ethical considerations. She may need her nephew to show her where all her TV channels are hiding, but she is a whiz with a new client check-in app.

The office looks very different now. Ellen sometimes thinks about adding more electrical outlets to accommodate it all. She is a reasonably sure that her new employee is surfing Facebook during staff meetings. At the same time, at the heart of the whole enterprise, Ellen is still leading a daily group for her clients.

The Impact of Cultural Change

Changing cultural beliefs and practices also shift human services professions. In 1969, Ellen may have been surprised by a "male nurse," but U.S. gender roles and expectations have changed in the half century since she first began working. Since the 1990s, Ellen has become much more sophisticated about multiculturalism and human diversity, and although she griped at the time, she now acknowledges that a new continuing education requirement for diversity training to maintain her chemical dependency certificate is a good idea. Ellen did not know any LGBTQ people in the 1970s, but she learned fast when the AIDS epidemic hit her city in the mid-1980s. When Ellen hired her first employee with a felony conviction and an addiction history to provide psychoeducational support, she worried that the state might shut down her agency. Now she makes a point of hiring as many people as she can who can serve as peer navigators and behavioral support specialists based on their own experiences of living with or successfully overcoming their issues.

Younger Ellen might have been aghast at some of Older Ellen's professional choices. Getting a certificate in drug treatment? You might as well just say you're knuckling under to the establishment. Buying a building? Owning private property? Locking the doors at night? Capitalism in action. Working with the police? Outrageous! But people change as well as the times, and Ellen can look back and see her professional choices in the context of her changing community and world view.

New Times, New Occupations

Many aspects of Ellen's job simply did not exist until recently. Although it has hard to imagine work today without a laptop or tablet, portable computers are a relatively new invention. Even portable phones used to be just phones, with no Internet connectivity. The idea of a webinar would mystify Ellen even at 40 years old.

New technology and new attitudes lead to new ways to provide human services. Continuing education and membership in professional organizations are two easy ways to keep up with employment trends and jobs just coming into being. According to one source, "The top 10 in-demand jobs in 2010 did not exist in 2004" (Ivy College, 2014), and another reflects, "Jobs exist now that we'd never heard of a decade ago. One estimate suggests that 65% of children entering primary school today will ultimately end up working in completely new job types that aren't on our radar yet" (Hallett & Hutt, 2016). Some of these new jobs are in or related to human services.

Human Services Is a Job Growth Area

Whether evaluated by the number of new positions or emerging occupations, human services is a robust field where job opportunities continue to expand. Remember that O*NET has a "bright occupations" page (National Center for O*NET Development, n.d.) where you can look at job growth areas (choose Rapid Growth from the dropdown menu and look for human services occupations). The Bureau of Labor Statistics (BLS)'s (2018b) "fastest growing occupations" page is another source of information on job growth, while the projections for most new jobs are found on an Occupational Outlook Handbook page (BLS, 2018c).

Look for emerging human services roles in chemical dependency, primary care and medical offices, geriatrics; with diverse populations; and in collaborative and cross-disciplinary settings.

You Change, Too!

As your career, life goals, and circumstances change, your job may change, too. Remember that you are likely to change jobs, and perhaps even careers, multiple times (Super,

Side Box 7.1

New Jobs in Human Services

These new occupations are directly related to the human services field or can be adapted to meet new human services demands. They did not exist before about 2000.

- App Designer
- Blogger
- Chief Listening Officer
- Data Scientist
- Educational or Admissions Consultant
- Elder Care Provider
- Lyft or Uber Driver
- Patient Advocate
- Market Research Data Miner
- Millennial Generational Expert
- Online Community or Content Manager
- Podcast Producer
- Senior Move Manager
- Social Media Manager
- Sustainability Director
- Telemedicine Physician
- Virtual Assistant
- Virtual Business Service Provider
- YouTube Content Creator (Vlogger)
- Zumba Teacher

(Burke, 2018; Casserly, 2012; Conlan, n.d.; Hallett & Hutt, 2016; King, 2013; Moore, 2017; Zupek, 2010)

How many of these jobs have you heard of? Do you know anyone working in these emerging professions? Read the sources for job descriptions and links, and use search terms like "jobs that didn't exist 10 years ago."

1980). BLS found that people born in the 1957–1964 cohort had an average of 11.7 jobs from 18 to 48 years old, with 27% having 15 or more jobs and 10% having 0–4 (BLS, 2018b). As BLS points out, this data may not be generalizable to people in other age cohorts, but they provide interesting statistics for comparison. BLS does not attempt to gauge how many times people change careers, since "no consensus has emerged on what constitutes a career change" (2018b). This is an important point. In the case study above, many of Ellen's roles and responsibilities changed, as did her credentials—but did her career change? Or did it just grow with her?

Your flexibility and adaptability will help you stay current in the field and qualified for as-yet-unknown roles. Will you be the first human services professional on Mars? Someday, you'll know the answer to this question.

Best of luck, from your first human services job onward!

Appendix A

National Organization for Human Services (NOHS)

National Organization for Human Services (NOHS) is a professional organization for students, faculty, staff, administrators, practitioners, and others involved in the human services field. Students can apply for membership at a reduced rate:

> A student is any individual who is currently enrolled in a course in human services or a closely related field (sociology, social work, counseling, psychology, etc.) and shares the goals and mission of NOHS. Students will be asked to submit the name of the current course(s) they are taking in human services and a contact number or email address of a faculty member with whom they are currently enrolled. *(NOHS, n.d.)*

Student awards and scholarships are available, as is membership in Tau Upsilon Alpha Honor Society (TUA, https://www.nationalhumanservices .org/tua).

NOHS holds a national continuing education and professional development conference annually. Students may submit proposals with the involvement of a faculty member. Students are eligible for a discounted conference rate.

NOHS regions also offer membership. Many also hold annual conferences. The regional conferences tend to be shorter, less expensive, and provide more opportunities for student involvement.

NOHS publishes a digital newsletter, conference proceedings, and the peer-reviewed *Journal of Human Services*.

NOHS members, including students, agree to adhere to NOHS's *Ethical Standards for Human Services Professionals* (see Appendix B). Human services academic programs may suggest or require students to follow these standards. Adherence to these ethical standards is required in programs accredited by the Council for Standards in Human Service Education (CSHSE).

Appendix B

NOHS *Ethical Standards for Human Services Professionals* (2015)

T he ethics code reprinted below is published on the website for the National Organization for Human Services. While some sections apply primarily to practitioners and faculty, many are relevant to student conduct, both in your program and at your field sites or in the community.

Preamble

Human services is a profession developed in response to the direction of human needs and human problems in the 1960's. Characterized by an appreciation of human beings in all of their diversity, human services offers assistance to its clients within the context of their communities and environments. Human service professionals and those who educate them promote and encourage the unique values and characteristics of human services. In so doing, human service professionals uphold the integrity and ethics of the profession, promote client and community well-being, and enhance their own professional growth.

The fundamental values of the human services profession include respecting the dignity and welfare of all people; promoting self-determination; honoring cultural diversity; advocating for social justice; and acting with integrity, honesty, genuineness and objectivity.

Human service professionals consider these standards in ethical and professional decision making. Conflicts may exist between this code and laws, workplace policies, cultural practices, credentialing boards, and personal beliefs. Ethical decision making processes should be employed to assure careful choices. Although ethical codes are not legal documents, they may be used to address issues related to the behavior of human service professionals.

Persons who use this code include members of the National Organization for Human Services, students in relevant academic degree programs, faculty in those same programs, researchers, administrators, and professionals in community agencies who identify with the profession of human services. The ethical standards are organized in sections around those persons to whom ethical practice should be applied.

Responsibility to Clients

STANDARD 1 Human service professionals recognize and build on client and community strengths.

STANDARD 2 Human service professionals obtain informed consent to provide services to clients at the beginning of the helping relationship. Clients should be informed that they may withdraw consent at any time except where denied by court order and should be able to ask questions before agreeing to the services. Clients who are unable to give consent should have those who are legally able to give consent for them review an informed consent statement and provide appropriate consent.

STANDARD 3 Human service professionals protect the client's right to privacy and confidentiality except when such confidentiality would cause serious harm to the client or others, when agency guidelines state otherwise, or under other stated conditions (e.g., local, state, or federal laws). Human service professionals inform clients of the limits of confidentiality prior to the onset of the helping relationship.

STANDARD 4 If it is suspected that danger or harm may occur to the client or to others as a result of a client's behavior, the human service professional acts in an appropriate and professional manner to protect the safety of those individuals. This may involve, but is not limited to, seeking consultation, supervision, and/or breaking the confidentiality of the relationship.

STANDARD 5 Human service professionals recognize that multiple relationships may increase the risk of harm to or exploitation of clients and may impair their professional judgment. When it is not feasible to avoid dual or multiple relationships, human service professionals should consider whether the professional relationship should be avoided or curtailed.

STANDARD 6 Sexual or romantic relationships with current clients are prohibited. Before engaging in sexual or romantic relationships with former clients, friends, or family members of former clients, human service professionals carefully evaluate potential exploitation or harm and refrain from entering into such a relationship.

STANDARD 7 Human service professionals ensure that their values or biases are not imposed upon their clients.

STANDARD 8 Human service professionals protect the integrity, safety, and security of client records. Client information in written or electronic form that is shared with other professionals must have the client's prior written consent except in the course of professional supervision or when legally obliged or permitted to share such information.

STANDARD 9 When providing services through the use of technology, human service professionals take precautions to ensure and maintain confidentiality and comply with all relevant laws and requirements regarding storing, transmitting, and retrieving data. In addition, human service professionals ensure that clients are aware of any issues and concerns related to confidentiality, service issues, and how technology might negatively or positively impact the helping relationship.

Responsibility to the Public and Society

STANDARD 10 Human service professionals provide services without discrimination or preference in regards to age, ethnicity, culture, race, ability, gender, language preference, religion, sexual orientation, socioeconomic status, nationality, or other historically oppressed groups.

STANDARD 11 Human service professionals are knowledgeable about their cultures and communities within which they practice. They are aware of multiculturalism in society and its impact on the community as well as individuals within the community. They respect the cultures and beliefs of individuals and groups.

STANDARD 12 Human service professionals are aware of local, state, and federal laws. They advocate for change in regulations and statutes when such legislation conflicts with ethical guidelines and/or client rights. Where laws are harmful to individuals, groups, or communities, human service professionals consider the conflict between the values of obeying the law and the values of serving people and may decide to initiate social action.

STANDARD 13 Human service professionals stay informed about current social issues as they affect clients and communities. If appropriate to the helping relationship, they share this information with clients, groups, and communities as part of their work.

STANDARD 14 Human service professionals are aware of social and political issues that differentially affect clients from diverse backgrounds.

STANDARD 15 Human service professionals provide a mechanism for identifying client needs and assets, calling attention to these needs and assets, and assisting in planning and mobilizing to advocate for those needs at the individual, community, and societal level when appropriate to the goals of the relationship.

STANDARD 16 Human service professionals advocate for social justice and seek to eliminate oppression. They raise awareness of underserved populations in their communities and with the legislative system.

STANDARD 17 Human service professionals accurately represent their qualifications to the public. This includes, but is not limited to, their abilities, training, education, credentials, academic endeavors, and areas of expertise. They avoid the appearance of misrepresentation or impropriety and take immediate steps to correct it if it occurs.

STANDARD 18 Human service professionals describe the effectiveness of treatment programs, interventions and treatments, and/or techniques accurately, supported by data whenever possible.

Responsibility to Colleagues

STANDARD 19 Human service professionals avoid duplicating another professional's helping relationship with a client. They consult with other professionals who are assisting the client in a different type of relationship when it is in the best interest of the client to do so. In addition, human services professionals seek ways to actively collaborate and coordinate with other professionals when appropriate.

STANDARD 20 When human service professionals have a conflict with a colleague, they first seek out the colleague in an attempt to manage the problem. If this effort fails, the professional then seeks the assistance of supervisors, consultants, or other professionals in efforts to address the conflict.

STANDARD 21 Human service professionals respond appropriately to unethical and problematic behavior of colleagues. Usually this means initially talking directly with the colleague and if no satisfactory resolution is achieved, reporting the colleague's behavior to supervisory or administrative staff.

STANDARD 22 All consultations between human service professionals are kept private, unless to do so would result in harm to clients or communities.

Responsibility to Employers

STANDARD 23 To the extent possible, human service professionals adhere to commitments made to their employers.

STANDARD 24 Human service professionals participate in efforts to establish and maintain employment conditions which are conducive to high quality client services. Whenever possible, they assist in evaluating the effectiveness of the agency through reliable and valid assessment measures.

STANDARD 25 When a conflict arises between fulfilling the responsibility to the employer and the responsibility to the client, human service professionals work with all involved to manage the conflict.

Responsibility to the Profession

STANDARD 26 Human service professionals seek the training, experience, education, and supervision necessary to ensure their effectiveness in working with culturally diverse individuals based on age, ethnicity, culture, race, ability, gender, language preference, religion, sexual orientation, socioeconomic status, nationality, or other historically oppressed groups. In addition, they will strive to increase their competence in methods which are known to be the best fit for the population(s) with whom they work.

STANDARD 27 Human service professionals know the limit and scope of their professional knowledge and offer services only within their knowledge, skill base, and scope of practice.

STANDARD 28 Human service professionals seek appropriate consultation and supervision to assist in decision-making when there are legal, ethical, or other dilemmas.

STANDARD 29 Human service professionals promote cooperation among related disciplines to foster professional growth and to optimize the impact of interprofessional collaboration on clients at all levels.

STANDARD 30 Human service professionals promote the continuing development of their profession. They encourage membership in professional associations, support research endeavors, foster educational advancement, advocate for appropriate legislative actions, and participate in other related professional activities.

STANDARD 31 Human service professionals continually seek out new and effective approaches to enhance their professional abilities and use techniques that are conceptually or evidence based. When practicing techniques that are experimental or new, they inform clients of the status of such techniques as well as the possible risks.

STANDARD 32 Human service professionals conduct research that adheres to all ethical principles, institutional standards, and scientific rigor. Such research takes into consideration cross-cultural bias and is reported in a manner that addresses any limitations.

STANDARD 33 Human service professionals make careful decisions about disclosing personal information while using social media, knowing that they reflect the profession of human services. In addition, they consider how their public conduct may reflect on themselves and their profession.

Responsibility to Self

STANDARD 34 Human service professionals are aware of their own cultural backgrounds, beliefs, values, and biases. They recognize the potential impact of their backgrounds on their relationships with others and work diligently to provide culturally competent service to all of their clients.

STANDARD 35 Human service professionals strive to develop and maintain healthy personal growth to ensure that they are capable of giving optimal services to clients. When they find that they are physically, emotionally, psychologically, or otherwise not able to offer such services, they identify alternative services for clients.

STANDARD 36 Human service professionals hold a commitment to lifelong learning and continually advance their knowledge and skills to serve clients more effectively.

Responsibility to Students

STANDARD 37 Human service educators develop and implement culturally sensitive knowledge, awareness, and teaching methodologies.

STANDARD 38 Human service educators are committed to the principles of access and inclusion and take all available and applicable steps to make education available to differently-abled students.

STANDARD 39 Human service educators demonstrate high standards of scholarship in their scholarship, pedagogy, and professional service and stay current in the field by being members of their professional associations, attending workshops and conferences, and reviewing and/or conducting research.

STANDARD 40 Human service educators recognize and acknowledge the contributions of students to the work of the educator in such activities as case material, grants, workshops, research, publications, and other related activities.

STANDARD 41 Human service educators monitor students' field experiences to ensure the quality of the placement site, supervisory experience, and learning experience towards the goals of personal, professional, academic, career, and civic development. When students experience potentially harmful events during field placements, educators provide reasonable investigation and response as necessary to safeguard the student.

STANDARD 42 Human service educators establish and uphold appropriate guidelines concerning student disclosure of sensitive/personal information which includes letting students have fair warning of any self-disclosure activities, allowing students to opt-out of in-depth self-disclosure activities when feasible, and ensuring that a mechanism is available to discuss and process such activities as needed.

STANDARD 43 Human service educators are aware that in their relationships with students, power, and status are unequal. Human service educators are responsible to clearly define and maintain ethical and professional relationships with students; avoid conduct that is demeaning, embarrassing, or exploitative of students; and always strive to treat students fairly, equally, and without discrimination.

STANDARD 44 Human service educators ensure students are familiar with, informed by, and accountable to the ethical standards and policies put forth by their program/department, the course syllabus/instructor, their advisor(s), and the Ethical Standards of Human Service Professionals.

Source: National Organization for Human Services. (2015). *Ethical Standards for Human Services Professionals.* Retrieved from https://www.nationalhumanservices.org/ethical-standards-for-hs-professionals

Appendix C

Center for Credentialing and Education Human Services–Board Certified Practitioner Certificate

Center for Credentialing and Education (CCE), an organization providing national and international training and certificates, offers certification options including the Human Services–Board Certified Practitioner (HS–BCP) credential. The HS–BCP (developed with assistance from NOHS) is available to graduates of an associate's program or higher. Certification includes an exam, which can be taken after graduation or while enrolled in a participating academic program. Also required is a review of your education, which can be in human services or other related fields with specific coursework, and a transcript, verification of your experience, and 350 hours of human services work experience after graduation. There is a process for people with degrees from outside the United States.

The HS–BCP qualifications and test areas are based on a national human services job analysis to ensure their relevance to practice in this field (Hinkle & O'Brien, 2010). HS–BCP certificate holders are required to follow the *HS–BCP Code of Ethics* (see Appendix D). CCE adjudicates ethics complaints.

You can look at the HS–BCP overview at http://www.cce-global.org/Credentialing/HSBCP, and see the application at http://www.cce-global.org/Assets/HSBCP/HSBCPApp.pdf.

CCE *HS–BCP Code of Ethics* (2009)

T he Center for Credentialing and Education (CCE) requires Human Services-Board Certified Practitioner (HS–BCP) certificate holders to adhere to a code of ethics. Because this is a certification related to human services practice, the ethical standards do not include sections on other aspects of a human services career, such as being a student or working as a faculty member. Instead, they generally focus on work with clients or clientele, or indirect services supporting this work, in a human services setting.

Unlike NOHS, whose ethics committee is not adjudicative, CCE has formal processes for evaluating an ethics complaint against an HS–BCP. CCE describes policies and procedures associated with ethics at http://www.cce-global.org/Credentialing/Ethics/HS-BCP.

Human Services-Board Certified Practitioner (HS-BCP) Code of Ethics

Introduction

The Human Services-Board Certified Practitioner (HS–BCP) is a credential created in a partnership between the Center for Credentialing and Education (CCE) and the National Organization for Human Services (NOHS), in consultation with the Council for Standards in Human Services Education (CSHSE). The credentialing program, administered by CCE, identifies qualified individuals who have satisfied the established knowledge standards.

Regardless of any other affiliations or credentials, this *HS–BCP Code of Ethics (Code)*, applies to each individual credentialed by CCE as a HS–BCP (credential holder), and each individual seeking HS–BCP credential (applicant). The *Code* is designed to provide appropriate ethics practice guidelines and enforceable standards of conduct for all credential holders and applicants. The *Code* also serves as a resource for those served by HS–BCP

credential holders and applicants (clients), with respect to such standards and requirements.

HS–BCP credential holders and applicants have the obligation to maintain high
standards of integrity and conduct; act in a manner that protects the welfare and interests of clients; accept responsibility for their actions; act consistent with accepted
ethical and legal standards; continually seek to enhance their occupational capabili-
ties; and practice with fairness and honesty.

Section A: Compliance With Legal Requirements and Conduct Standards

HS–BCP credential holders and applicants shall:

1. Comply with all applicable laws and governmental regulations relating to occupational activities.
2. Refrain from other conduct or behavior that is contrary to legal, occupational,
   ethical standards or requirements.
3. Refrain from behavior involving dishonesty, fraud, deceit, or misrepresentation.
4. Refrain from unlawful discrimination in occupational activities, including but not
   limited to discrimination based on age, race, gender, ethnicity, sexual orientation,
   gender orientation, religion, national origin, or disability. Occupational activities
   include relationships with employers, clients, and colleagues.
5. Avoid condoning or engaging in harassment, including but not limited to deliber-
   ate or repeated unwelcome comments, gestures, or physical contact.
6. Maintain accurate and otherwise appropriate client records in accordance with
   applicable legal and occupational requirements.
7. Make appropriate disclosures and referrals to government agencies and employers
   when a client appears to be a danger or is otherwise unable to act safely concerning him/herself or others. Such disclosures and referrals shall be consistent with
   legal and occupational requirements.

Section B: Compliance With CCE Organizational Policies and Rules

HS–BCP credential holders and applicants shall:

1. Comply with all applicable CCE policies and procedures, including the *HS–BCP
   Code of Ethics* and CCE *Ethics Case Procedures,* as amended or revised.
2. Provide accurate information to CCE.
3. Maintain the security of confidential CCE information and materials.
4. Cooperate fully with CCE concerning ethics matters, including the collection of
   information.
5. Inform and support others regarding certification standards and responsibilities
   set forth in this *Code.*

6. Report an apparent violation of the *HS–BCP Code of Ethics* by a credential holder or applicant upon a reasonable and clear factual basis.

Section C: Performance of Services and Other Occupational Activities

HS–BCP credential holders and applicants shall:

1. Conduct all occupational activities responsibly and fairly with employers, clients, and colleagues.

2. Recognize the scope and limitations of their respective occupational abilities and qualifications, and provide services only when qualified. Each credential holder or applicant is responsible for determining the limits of his or her own abilities based on education, knowledge, skills, practice experience, credentials, and other relevant considerations.

3. Maintain and protect the confidentiality of private or otherwise sensitive information obtained in the course of providing services unless the information is reasonably understood to pertain to an unlawful activity, a court, or governmental agency lawfully directs the release of the confidential information or the employer or client expressly authorizes the release of specific confidential information.

4. Properly use occupational credentials, titles, and degrees; and provide truthful and accurate representations concerning education, experience, qualifications, competency, and the performance of services.

5. Avoid occupational techniques that are harmful to clients. Each credential holder or applicant is responsible for ensuring that the techniques used are consistent with clients' needs, emotional, intellectual and physical capacities; and shall inform clients regarding the purpose, application, and results of the occupational techniques, assessments, and strategies.

6. Obtain clients' informed consent before initiating a relationship and throughout the duration of the relationship. Each credential holder or applicant shall discuss the purposes, goals, and nature of the relationship, as well as the limits of confidentiality and privacy.

7. Seek consultation or supervision with qualified service providers when unable to provide appropriate assistance to a client, and provide appropriate referrals when terminating a service relationship.

Section D: Avoidance of Conflicts of Interest and the Appearance of Impropriety

HS–BCP credential holders and applicants shall:

1. Disclose to employers or clients significant circumstances that could be construed as a potential or real conflict of interest, or any having an appearance of impropriety.

2. Avoid conduct that could cause a conflict of interest related to, or otherwise interfere with, occupational judgments regarding a client or employer. If such a circumstance is unavoidable, the credential holder or applicant shall take reasonable steps to resolve such conflict.

3. Avoid engaging in multiple relationships with clients. In situations where multiple relationships cannot be avoided, the credential holder or applicant shall discuss the potential effects of the relationships with the affected client(s), and shall take reasonable steps to avoid any harm to the client(s).

4. Avoid sexual or romantic relationships with current clients. Credential holders and applicants do not engage in sexual or romantic interactions with former clients for a minimum of two (2) years following the last HS–BCP contact.

5. Refrain from offering or accepting significant payments, gifts, or other forms of compensation or benefits that are intended to influence occupational judgment.

6. Accurately, truthfully, and completely acknowledge the intellectual property of others with respect to all activities.

Appendix E

National Association of Social Workers (NASW)

The National Association of Social Workers (NASW) is a professional organization for social workers, social work students, and those associated with social work (NASW, 2018a). Social work students and students in other fields can apply for student membership at a reduced rate. Associate membership "is open to anyone who has a professional interest in, or is supportive of, the issues addressed by, or the client populations served by, the social work profession" (NASW, 2018b). The dues include membership in the national organization and your local chapter.

NASW's webpage includes a section on student resources (NASW, 2018c). Student awards and scholarships are available.

NASW and its chapters hold continuing education and professional development conferences annually. Students are eligible for discounted conference rates.

NASW publishes a monthly newsletter, several peer-reviewed journals, and other publications and resources.

NASW members, including students, agree to adhere to NASW's *Code of Ethics* (see Appendix F). Social work academic programs may suggest or require students to follow these standards. NASW reviews the ethical conduct of its members.

National Association of Social Workers (NASW)

Appendix F

NASW Code of Ethics (2017)

N ASW members, including students, must adhere to NASW's *Code of Ethics* (NASW, 2016, 2017). This includes members who are not licensed as social workers. NASW offers ethics consultation and reviews ethics complaints against members.

The code is divided into four sections. *Ethical Principles* includes broad guiding standards of the profession. *Ethical Standards* includes six categories, each including multiple standards, such as Sexual Relationships, and Continuing Education and Staff Development.

The code was revised in 2017 to include enhanced ethical considerations related to technology.

The main divisions of the code are:

+ Preamble
+ Purpose of the NASW *Code of Ethics*
+ Ethical Principles
+ Ethical Standards
    1. Social Workers' Ethical Responsibilities to Clients
    2. Social Workers' Ethical Responsibilities to Colleagues
    3. Social Workers' Ethical Responsibilities in Practice Settings
    4. Social Workers' Ethical Responsibilities as Professionals
    5. Social Workers' Ethical Responsibilities to the Social Work Profession
    6. Social Workers' Ethical Responsibilities to the Broader Society

Full code available at: National Association of Social Workers. (2017). Code of ethics [2017 revision]. https://www.socialworkers.org/About/Ethics/Code-of-Ethics/Code-of-Ethics-English

Appendix G

NAADAC

NAADAC: The Association for Addiction Professionals is a professional organization that offers training, continuing education, and information on national certification as an addictions professional through the National Certification Commission for Addiction Professionals (NCC AP). Their website, https://www.naadac.org/, includes resources such as information on different states' licensure or certification requirements in the addictions field (NAADAC, n.d.).

NAADAC publishes a newsletter, a magazine, and other publications. It holds and advertises conferences, in-person and online trainings, and events.

You can become a student member of NAADAC. Other membership categories are available if you are working in the addictions or recovery field, are active military, or live and work internationally.

NAADAC also has career and resources pages and its own ethics code, the *NAADAC/NCC AP Code of Ethics* (see Appendix H).

Appendix H

NAADAC/NCC AP *Code of Ethics* (2016)

NAADAC: The Association for Addiction Professionals and the National Certification Commission for Addiction Professionals (NCC AP) provide ethical standards for addictions interventionists. These are the standards for professionals with national addictions certification through NCC AP, and may be the standards required by your state certifying entity as well.

This set of ethical standards is specific to addictions intervention, which, of course, includes ethics related to general issues such as confidentiality, record keeping, competence, and other aspects associated with human services intervention.

This code is spelled out in great detail—it runs to 21 pages in its current version. The standards are grouped under these sections:

+ Introduction to NAADAC/NCC AP Ethical Standards
+ Principle I: The Counseling Relationship
+ Principle II: Confidentiality and Privileged Communication
+ Principle III: Professional Responsibilities and Workplace Standards
+ Principle IV: Working in a Culturally Diverse World
+ Principle V: Assessment, Evaluation, and Interpretation
+ Principle VI: E-Therapy, E-Supervision, and Social Media
+ Principle VII: Supervision and Consultation
+ Principle VIII: Resolving Ethical Concerns
+ Principle IX: Research and Publication

A general introduction to this code appears at https://www.naadac.org/code-of-ethics, which also includes links to the code in PDF and HTML formats.

Appendix I

Online Career and Self-Knowledge Tests and Tools

This list includes resources described in Chapters 1 and 2. If possible, start with your career center. Using career center and career counseling resources will be more efficient and decrease the chance of misinterpreting or being distressed by your results. It may also reduce or eliminate the fees associated with some tests.

If you use these resources on your own and have questions or concerns about your results, seek consultation from a career counselor or other person familiar with these tests.

Consolidated Sites

+ The Balance Careers
  https://www.thebalancecareers.com/free-career-aptitude-tests-2059813
+ The Muse Editor: The 11 Best Career Quizzes to Help You Find Your Dream Job
  https://www.themuse.com/advice/the-11-best-career-quizzes-to-help-you-find-your-dream-job
+ MyPlan.com
  https://www.myplan.com/

Test-Specific Sites

+ Assessment.com: MAPP™ Career Assessment Test
  https://www.assessment.com/AboutMAPP
+ CAS Career Assessment Site: The FIRO-B® Test
  https://careerassessmentsite.com/tests/firo-business-firo-b-tests/about-the-firo-b/
+ OutOfService: The Big Five Project Personality Test
  https://www.outofservice.com/bigfive/

- PAR: Self-Directed Search
  http://www.self-directed-search.com/
- Truity: The Big Five Personality Test
  https://www.truity.com/test/big-five-personality-test

References

ACES Too High. (n.d.). Got your ACE score? Retrieved from https://acestoohigh.com/got-your-ace-score/

Alle-Corliss, L. A., & Alle-Corliss, R. M. (2005). *Human service agencies: An orientation to fieldwork* (2nd ed.). Boston, MA: Cengage.

Alther, L. (1982). *Other women*. New York, NY: Plume.

American Counseling Association. (2014). ACA code of ethics. Retrieved from https://www.counseling.org/resources/aca-code-of-ethics.pdf

American Psychological Association. (2017). Ethical principles of psychologists and code of conduct. Retrieved from www.apa.org/ethics/code/

American Psychological Association. (2018). "How did you get that job?" Retrieved from http://www.apa.org/members/your-growth/career-development/how-did-you-get-that-job/index.aspx

Assessment.com. (n.d.). MAPP™ career assessment test. Retrieved from https://www.assessment.com/AboutMAPP

Baird, B. (2016). *Internship, practicum, and field placement handbook* (7th ed.). New York, NY: Routledge.

The Balance Careers. (n.d.). [Home page]. Retrieved from https://www.thebalancecareers.com/free-career-aptitude-tests-2059813

Bolles, R. N. (2018). *What color is your parachute? 2019: A practical manual for job-hunters and career-changers*. New York, NY: Ten Speed Press.

Bronfenbrenner, U. (1989). Ecological systems theory. *Annals of Child Development, 6*, 187–249.

Bureau of Labor Statistics (BLS). (2011). Helping those in need: Human service workers. Retrieved from https://www.bls.gov/careeroutlook/2011/fall/art03.pdf

Bureau of Labor Statistics (BLS). (2018a). Economic news release. Retrieved from https://www.bls.gov/bls/newsrels.htm

Bureau of Labor Statistics (BLS). (2018b). Fastest growing occupations. Retrieved from https://www.bls.gov/emp/tables/fastest-growing-occupations

Bureau of Labor Statistics (BLS). (2018c). Occupational outlook handbook. Retrieved from https://www.bls.gov/ooh/

Burger, W. R., Youkeles, M., Malamet, F. B., Smith, F. B., & Guigno, C. (2000). *The helping professions: A careers sourcebook*. Boston, MA: Cengage.

Burke, Z. (2018). 10 jobs that didn't exist 10 years ago. Retrieved from https://digitalmarketing institute.com/en-us/blog/10-jobs-didnt-exist-10-years-ago

Carrol, M. (2006). *Awake at work: 35 practical Buddhist principles for discovering clarity and balance in the midst of work's chaos.* Boulder, CO: Shambhala.

Career Assessment Site. (2017). The FIRO-B® test. Retrieved from https://careerassessmentsite. com/tests/firo-business-firo-b-tests/about-the-firo-b/

Casserly, M. (2012, May 11). 10 jobs that didn't exist 10 years ago. Retrieved from https:// www.forbes.com/sites/meghancasserly/2012/05/11/10-jobs-that-didnt-exist-10-years-ago/#527173d557ba

Center for Credentialing and Education (CCE). (2009). *Human Services–Board Certified Practitioner Code of ethics.* Retrieved from http://www.cce-global.org/Assets/Ethics/HSBCPcodeofethics.pdf

Center for Credentialing and Education (CCE). (2016a). HS-BCP Human Services–Board Certified Practitioner. Retrieved from http://www.cce-global.org/hsbcp

Center for Credentialing & Education (CCE). (2016b). Human Services–Board Certified Practitioner. Retrieved from http://www.cce-global.org/Credentialing/HSBCP

Center for Credentialing & Education (CCE). (2016c). Human Services–Board Certified Practitioner application packet. Retrieved from http://www.cce-global.org/Assets/HSBCP/HSBCPApp.pdf

Center for Credentialing and Education (CCE). (2016d). Policies and procedures. Retrieved from http://www.cce-global.org/Credentialing/Ethics/HS-BCP

Centers for Disease Control. (2016, April 1). Adverse childhood experiences (ACEs). Retrieved from https://www.cdc.gov/violenceprevention/acestudy/index.html

Charity Navigator. (2018). [Home page.] Retrieved from https://www.charitynavigator.org/

Chronister, K. M., McWhirter, B. T., & Kerewsky, S. D. (2004). Prevention from an ecological framework. In R. K. Conyne & E. P. (Eds.), *Ecological counseling: An innovative approach to conceptualizing person-environment interaction* (pp. 315–338). Alexandria, VA: American Counseling Association Press.

Clay, R. A. (2012). 20 years of advancing mental and behavioral health. Retrieved from http://www.apa.org/monitor/2012/12/20-years.aspx

Collison, B. B., & Garfield, N. J. (Eds.). (1996). *Careers in counseling and human services* (2nd ed.). Washington, D.D.: Taylor & Francis.

Conlan, C. (n.d.). 5 high-paying jobs that didn't exist 10 years ago. https://www.monster.com/career-advice/article/jobs-that-did-not-exist

Conlan, C. (2018). 10 awesome free career self-assessment tools on the Internet. Retrieved from https://www.monster.com/career-advice/article/best-free-career-assessment-tools

Council for Standards in Human Service Education (CSHSE). (2010). Retrieved from http://www.cshse.org/

Council for Standards in Human Service Education (CSHSE). (2018). *CSHSE member handbook: Self-study and accreditation guide July 2018.* Retrieved from https://cshse.org/wp-content/uploads/2018/07/CSHSE-Member-Handbook-Accreditation-and-Self-Study-Guide-July-2018.pdf

Courts for Kids. (2018). [Home page]. Retrieved from http://courtsforkids.org/

DiMarco, C. (1997). *Career transitions: A journey of survival and growth.* Scottsdale, AZ: Gorsuch Scarisbrick.

Doyle, A. (2018). What is the occupational outlook handbook? Retrieved from https://www.thebalancecareers.com/what-is-the-occupational-outlook-handbook-2058465

eHealth. (2018). History and timeline of the Affordable Care Act (ACA). Retrieved from https://www.ehealthinsurance.com/resources/affordable-care-act/history-timeline-affordable-care-act-aca

Galindo, I., Boomer, E., & Reagan, D. (2006). *A family genogram workbook.* Kearney, NJ: Educational Consultants.

Genopro. (n.d.). Introduction to the genogram. Retrieved from https://www.genopro.com/genogram/

Ginzberg, E., Ginsburg, S., Axelrad, S., & Herma, J. (1951). *Occupational choice: An approach to a general theory.* New York, NY: Columbia University Press.

Glassdoor. (2018). Human services specialist interview. Retrieved from https://www.glassdoor.com/Interview/human-services-specialist-interview-questions-SRCH_KO0,25.htm

Gorski, P. C. (1995–2015). Circles of my multicultural self. Retrieved from http://www.edchange.org/multicultural/activities/circlesofself.html

Guidestar. (2018). [Home page.] Retrieved from https://www.guidestar.org

Haelle, T. (2018, July 9). Burnout tied to twofold higher risk for medical errors. Retrieved from https://www.medscape.com/viewarticle/899053

Hallett, R., & Hutt, R. (2016, June 7). 10 jobs that didn't exist 10 years ago. Retrieved from https://www.weforum.org/agenda/2016/06/10-jobs-that-didn-t-exist-10-years-ago/

Hays, P. A. (2016). *Addressing cultural complexities in practice: Assessment, diagnosis, and therapy* (3rd ed.). Washington, DC: American Psychological Association.

Hinkle, J. S., & O'Brien, S. (2010). The Human Services–Board Certified Practitioner: An overview of a new national credential. *Journal of Human Services, 30*(1), 23–28. Retrieved from https://www.nationalhumanservices.org/assets/Journal/2010.pdf.

Hloom. (2018). Free Microsoft Office templates. Retrieved from https://www.hloom.com/

Howard, P. J., and Howard, J. M. (2000). *The owner's manual for personality at work: How the Big Five personality traits affect your performance, communication, teamwork, leadership, and sales.* Austin, TX: Bard Press.

The Inside-Out Prison Exchange Program®. (2018). The Inside-Out Prison Exchange Program®: Social change through transformative education. Retrieved from http://www.insideoutcenter.org/

Irwin, N. (2018, September 7). The economy needs more workers: Last month, it got fewer. *The New York Times.* Retrieved from https://www.nytimes.com/2018/09/07/upshot/jobs-report-economy-needs-workers.html

Ivey, A. E., Ivey, M. B., & Zalaquett, C. P. (2018). *Intentional interviewing and counseling: Facilitating client development in a multicultural society* (9th ed.). Boston, MA: Cengage.

Ivy College. (2014, May 7) We are living in exponential times [Web log post]. Retrieved from https://www.ivy.edu.au/blog/career-and-study-advice/living-exponential-times/

Kabat-Zinn, J. (2013). *Full catastrophe living: Using the wisdom of your body and mind to face stress, pain, and illness* (Rev. ed.) New York, NY: Bantam.

Kerewsky, S. D. (Ed.). (2016). *Fitness for the human services profession: Preliminary explorations* [Edited monograph]. Alexandria, VA: Council for Standards in Human Service Education.

Kerewsky, S. D., & Geiken, L. (2007). "Have you got what it takes to train security trolls?" Career counseling for wizards. In N. Mulholland (Ed.), *The psychology of Harry Potter: An unauthorized examination of the boy who lived* (pp. 45–57). Dallas, TX: BenBella Books.

King, M. (2013, April 4). Five jobs that didn't exist 10 years ago. Retrieved from https://www.businessinsider.com/five-jobs-that-didnt-exist-10-years-ago-2013-4

Kiser, P. M. (2015). *The human services internship: Getting the most from your experience* (4th ed.). Boston, MA: Cengage.

Kliman, J. (2010, Winter,). Intersections of social privilege and marginalization: A visual teaching tool. *AFTA Monograph Series*, 39–48.

Landrum, R. E. (2009). *Finding jobs with a psychology bachelor's degree: Expert advice for launching your career*. Washington, DC: American Psychological Association.

Lent, R. W., Brown, S. D., & Hackett, G. (1994). Toward a unified social cognitive theory of career/academic interest, choice, and performance. *Journal of Vocational Behavior, 45*, 79–122.

Lent, R. W., Brown, S. D., & Hackett, G. (2000). Contextual supports and barriers to career choice: A social cognitive analysis. *Journal of Counseling Psychology, 47*, 36–49.

Lichtenstein, D. P., Lindstrom, L. E., & Kerewsky, S. D. (2005). A delicate balance: An integrated model for the preparation of ethically competent human services professionals. *Human Service Education, 25*(1), 27–39.

LinkedIn. (2018). [Home page]. Retrieved from https://www.linkedin.com

Luft, J., & Ingham, H. (1955). The Johari Window: A graphic model for interpersonal relations. *Proceedings of the Western Training Laboratory in Group Development*. Los Angeles, CA: University of California, Los Angeles.

Mayeda, P. N., & Friendship with Cambodia. (2017). Responsible travel guide Cambodia: Improving lives through thoughtful travel choices (2nd ed). Eugene, OR: Wild Iris.

McGoldrick, M., Gerson, R., & Shellenberger, S. (1999). *Genograms: Assessment and intervention* (2nd updated edition). New York, NY: Norton.

McWhirter, J. J., McWhirter, B. T., McWhirter, E. H., & McWhirter, A. C. (2017). *At risk youth: A comprehensive response for counselors, teachers, psychologists, and human service professionals*. Boston, MA: Cengage.

Melton, S. H. (2017, September 6). 3 Steps to minimize burnout. Retrieved from https://www.medscape.com/viewarticle/884445

Meyers & Briggs Foundation. (n.d.). [Home page]. Retrieved from http://www.myersbriggs.org/

Monster. (2018). [Home page]. Retrieved from https://www.monster.com

Moore, E. (2017, October 23). 5 awesome jobs that didn't exist 15 years ago. Retrieved from https://www.glassdoor.com/blog/jobs-that-didnt-exist-15-years-ago/

Muse Editor. (2018). The 11 best career quizzes to help you find your dream job. Retrieved from https://www.themuse.com/advice/the-11-best-career-quizzes-to-help-you-find-your-dream-job

Myers, I. B., & Myers, P. B. (1995). *Gifts differing: Understanding personality type* (Reprint ed.). Mountain View, CA: Davies-Black.

MyPlan.com. (2004-2018). [Home page]. Retrieved from https://www.myplan.com/

NAADAC: Association for Addictions Professionals. (n.d.). [Home page]. Retrieved from https://www.naadac.org/

NAADAC: Association for Addictions Professionals. (2016). Introduction to NAADAC/NCC AP ethical standards. Retrieved from https://www.naadac.org/code-of-ethics

National Alliance on Mental Illness (NAMI) (2018). [Home page]. Retrieved from https://www.nami.org/

National Association of Social Workers (NASW). (2016). Code of ethics [Main page]. Available from https://www.socialworkers.org/About/Ethics/Code-of-Ethics

National Association of Social Workers (NASW). (2017). Code of ethics [2017 revision]. Retrieved from https://www.socialworkers.org/About/Ethics/Code-of-Ethics/Code-of-Ethics-English

National Association of Social Workers (NASW). (2018a). [Home page]. Available from https://www.socialworkers.org

National Association of Social Workers (NASW). (2018b). Membership types & annual dues. Available from https://www.socialworkers.org/Membership/Membership-Types

National Association of Social Workers (NASW). (2018c). Resources for students. Available from https://www.socialworkers.org/Careers/Career-Center/Resources-for-Students

National Center for O*NET Development. (n.d.a). O*NET interest profiler. Retrieved from https://www.mynextmove.org/explore/ip

National Center for O*NET Development. (n.d.b). Skills search. Retrieved from https://www.onetonline.org/search/ https://www.onetonline.org/skills/

National Center for O*NET Development. (n.d.c). Work values. Retrieved from https://www.onetonline.org/find/descriptor/browse/Work_Values/

National Center for O*NET Development. (n.d.d) Bright outlook occupations. Retrieved from https://www.onetonline.org/help/bright/

National Center for O*NET Development. (2018). O*NET Online. Retrieved from https://www.onetonline.org/

National Organization for Human Services. (n.d.a). [Home page]. Retrieved from http://www.nationalhumanservices.org/

National Organization for Human Services. (n.d.b). Tau Upsilon Alpha Honor Society. Retrieved from https://www.nationalhumanservices.org/tua

National Organization for Human Services. (2015). *Ethical Standards for Human Services Professionals.* Retrieved from https://www.nationalhumanservices.org/ethical-standards-for-hs-professionals

Neukrug, E., Kalkbrenner, M., & Snow, K. (2017). *Dictionary of counseling & human services: An essential resource for students and professional helpers.* Norfolk, VA: Counseling Books Etc.

OutOfService. (n.d.). The Big Five project personality test. Retrieved from https://www.outofservice.com/bigfive/

PAR. (2018a). Self-directed search. Retrieved from http://www.self-directed-search.com/

PAR. (2018b). RIASEC theory. Retrieved from http://www.self-directed-search.com/How-does-it-work/RIASEC-theory

PAR. (2018c). SDS case studies. Retrieved from http://www.self-directed-search.com/Who-Uses-It/Case-Studies

Parsons, K. A. (2015). Human services historical timeline. Retrieved from https://prezi.com/2qix1nprrsry/human-services-historical-timeline/

Psychological Assessment, Consultation, and Education Services (PACES). (n.d.). [Home page]. Retrieved from https://www.pacespsych.com/

Quinsigamond Community College. (2018). Brief history of human service education. Retrieved from https://www.qcc.edu/human-services/history

Rowling, J. K. (1998). *Harry Potter and the sorcerer's stone.* New York, NY: Scholastic.

Rowling, J. K. (2003). *Harry Potter and the chamber of secrets.* New York, NY: Scholastic.

Sapolsky, R. M. (2004). *Why zebras don't get ulcers* (3rd ed.). New York, NY: Henry Holt.

Semester at Sea. (2018). [Home page]. Retrieved from https://www.semesteratsea.org/

Shallcross, L. (January 1, 2013). Making life work. *Counseling Today,* 34–41. Retrieved from https://ct.counseling.org/2013/01/making-life-work/

Shally-Jensen, M. (Ed.). (2015). *Careers in human services.* Hackensack, NJ: Salem.

State of Minnesota. (2018). Careeronestop. Retrieved from https://www.careeronestop.org/

Substance Abuse and Mental Health Services. (2017, September 5). Adverse childhood experiences. Retrieved from https://www.samhsa.gov/capt/practicing-effective-prevention/prevention-behavioral-health/adverse-childhood-experiences

Super, D. E. (1980). A life-span, life-space approach to career development. *Journal of Vocational Behavior, 16,* 282–298. doi:10.1016/0001-8791(80)90056-1

Sweitzer, H. F., & King, M. A. (2014). *The successful internship: Personal, professional, and civic development in experiential learning* (4th ed.). Belmont, CA: Brooks/Cole Cengage.

Truity. (2017). The Big Five Personality Test. Retrieved from https://www.truity.com/test/big-five-personality-test

Tuma, R. S. (2017, October 23). Simple tool shows lasting reduction in burnout. Retrieved from https://www.medscape.com/viewarticle/887432?nlid=118701_4503andsrc=wnl_dne_171024_mscpeditanduac=140598EYandimpID=1463755andfaf=1

University of Missouri. (2018). Career interests game. Retrieved from https://career.missouri.edu/career-interest-game/

VocBio Vocational Biographies. (n.d.). [Home page]. Retrieved from https://www.vocbio.com/

Wagner, B. C., & DuBasky, V. (2002). *Soul survivors: Stories of women and children in Cambodia.* 2nd edition. Eugene, OR: Wild Iris.

Williams, J. P. (2018, May 1). Report: Obamacare coverage gains are eroding. Retrieved from https://www.usnews.com/news/healthiest-communities/articles/2018-05-01/obamacare-gains-in-insurance-coverage-starting-to-erode-report-says

Winbolt, B. (2003). *Brief manual: Solution focused brief therapy* [Kindle ed.]. ISR Publishing.

Workbloom. (2006-2018). Human services resume. Retrieved from https://workbloom.com/resume/sample/human-services.aspx

Yale University Office of Career Strategy. (n.d.). CV -> resume conversion guide. Retrieved from https://ocs.yale.edu/sites/default/files/files/CV%20to%20ResumeWorkshopfinal.pdf

Zupek, R. (2010, January 14). 10 careers that didn't exist 10 years ago. Retrieved from https://www.aol.com/2010/01/14/careers-that-didnt-exist-10-years-ago/

Index

A

academic advisors, 42–43
ACE questionnaire, 34
ADDRESSING Framework, 20–22
adoption case manager, 48
Adverse Childhood Experiences Study (ACES), 34
Affordable Care Act (ACA), 2
Agreeableness, 30
alumni/ae, 54–55
American Counseling Association (ACA), 7
American Psychological Association (APA), 7
ethics code, 6
application, sending, 106
Assessment.com, 17
associate's-level human services, 2
associate's-level licensure and certification, 115–116
Awake at Work: 35 Practical Buddhist Principles for Discovering Clarity and Balance in the Midst of Work's Chaos (Michael Carroll), 35

B

bachelor's-level human services, 2, 6–7
bachelor's-level licensure and certification, 115–116
Basic Listening Sequence (BLS), 12
Big Five Personality Test, 18, 30, 94
free versions of, 30
Black Student Union, 43
Bright Outlook Occupations, 15
Bronfenbrenner's Ecological Model, 24–25
Bureau of Labor Statistics (BLS), 2–3
employment projections, 3
burnout, 34–35
medical errors and, 35
self-care and avoiding, 34–35
suggestion for reversing, 35

C

California Personality Inventory (CPI), 20
campus resources, 18
campus supervisor, 11
capstone project, 41, 58
career centers, 13, 66, 91–92
career counseling for self-exploration, 26
career counselors, 13
career development, 59–61
career exploration, 13
Careeronestop, 17
career options in human services, 59–61
career self-evaluation, 20
activities for informal exploration, 20
understanding triggers and vulnerabilities, 31
career self-evaluation, tools for
ADDRESSING Framework, 20–22
Bronfenbrenner's Ecological Model, 24–25
genogram, 22–23
Johari Window, 23–24
Kliman's Social Matrix, 22
career self-reflection, questions for, 36–37
Career Stories, 68
career strengths, evaluation of, 26–31
CCE HS–BCP Code of Ethics, 137–140
Center for Credentialing and Education (CCE), 40, 135
Center for Credentialing and Education's (CCE) Human Services–Board Certified Practitioner certificate, 117
certificates, 6
certification requirements, 115–117
Charity Navigator, 93
CHIP (Children's Health Insurance Program), 2
Circles of My Multicultural Self, 5
client confidentiality, 102
client welfare, 8
college websites, 43

common job requirements, 49–50
community care, 2
competence, 8
confidentiality, 6, 8
conflict resolution, 7
Conscientiousness, 30
continuing education, 124
cooperative education placement, 41, 45
Council for Standards in Human Service Education (CSHSE), 40
counseling, 36
countertransference, 5, 31–33
in long-term therapy relationship, 33
cover letters, 103–105
curriculum vitae (CV), 98, 112
accuracy and honesty in, 102
format and ways of describing experiences, 100
presentation listing styles, 101
professional email address, use of, 100
templates, 96–97
vs resume, 57, 96, 98–99
CV to Resume Conversion Guide, 105

D

deinstitutionalization, 2
direct human service roles, 62–63
direct service jobs, 61–62
direct service providers, characteristics of, 62–64
disclosing a felony, 116

E

employment ads, 55
ethics in human services, 6–9, 129–134, 143
CCE HS–BCP Code of Ethics, 137–140
client welfare, 8
competence, 8
confidentiality, 8
job interview, case example, 10
licenses and certificates, 6
multiple-role relationships, 8

relationship between laws and
  ethics, 6
requirements of agencies, academic
  programs, and professional
  organizations, 6–7
scope of practice, 6
ethnicity, 20
externship, 41, 45
Extraversion, 30

F

Facebook, 17
field placements, 47–48
field site supervisor, 11
Finding Jobs with a Psychology
  Bachelor's Degree: Expert
  Advice for Launching Your
  Career, 91
FIRO-B*, 18, 26, 29
  pairing with MBTI*, 29
first-generation college students, 45
flexible, being, 57–58
fostered services, 1
free online career and preference
  tests, 30
Full Catastrophe Living: Using the
  Wisdom of Your Body and
  Mind to Face Stress, Pain, and
  Illness (Jon Kabat-Zinn), 35

G

gatekeeping function, 9–11
gender, 20
genogram, 22–23
Gifts Differing: Understanding
  Personality Type, 29
graduate programs, 118
Guidestar, 93

H

Hays, Pamela, 20
helping services, 1
Hloom, 105
Holland Codes, 16, 61
human diversity and culture, 5
human services
  careers in, 3–4
  cultural change, impact of,
    123–124
  definition, 1
  diversity and, 5
  ethics in, 6–9
  future of, 121–123
  job opportunities in, 124–126
  knowledge and skills, 12
  occupations, 2
  overview of contemporary, 1–2
  professionals, 2
  reasons for entering, 19–20
  related undergraduate degrees,
    2–3
  technology, impact of, 123

Human Services–Board Certified Practitioner (HS–BCP)
  credentials, 7, 40, 135
human services internship
  handbooks, 52
human services portfolios, 105
human services trainings and
  conferences, 94
human services trajectory, 87–89

I

indirect human service roles, 65
indirect service jobs, 64
indirect service providers,
  characteristics of, 64
"informed consent for being a
  student", 40–42
Inside-Out Prison Exchange
  Program*, 53
institutional resources, 39–45
international field placements, 66
international internships, 66
internships, 41, 45
  human services internship
    handbooks, 52
  international, 66
  noncredit, 66
  postdegree international, 67
interview questions, 109
interviews with human services
  students and professionals,
    69–87
  Akiko, 73–75
  Bhavia Wagner, 84–87
  common and differing elements
    of, 89
  David Gardiepy, 82–84
  Diane, 71–73
  Jade, 75–76
  Moira, 69–71
  Niki, 76–80
  Rachel, 80–82
introverted person, 26

J

job announcements, 68, 112
  checklist for, 93
  finding, 92
  language, 101–102
  tailoring resume to, 101
job application errors and problems,
  tips for avoiding, 118–119
job-based site placement strategy,
  48
job characteristics, 60
job-finding resources, 13, 91–92
job interviews, 106
  interview questions, 109
  online considerations, 107
  organizing oneself, 108
  preparation for, 107–108
  professional attire, 108
  telephone and voice mail
    considerations, 107
job search

human services trainings and
  conferences, 94–95
job announcements, 68, 92
posting credentials online,
  95–96
preparing for, 112–113
resources for, 91–92
suggestions for attuning, 119
job supervisor, 11
Johari Window, 23–24

K

Kliman's Social Matrix, 22

L

laws, relationship between ethics
  and, 6
legal record, 116
licenses, 6
licensure requirements, 115–116
LinkedIn, 95

M

master's of social work (MSW), 6
MBTI*
  FIRO-B* pairing with, 29
Medical Assistants, 15
Medicare, 2
membership in professional
  organizations, 95
Monster Worldwide, 17
multiculturalism, 5
multiple-role relationships, 7–8
Myers-Briggs Type Indicator*
  (MBTI*), 18, 26–30, 61
  case study, 27–28
  personality types, 26
  preference types, 26
  resources, 29
MyPlan.com, 17

N

NAADAC, 117, 145
NAADAC-NCC AP ethics code,
  6, 147
National Association of Social Workers (NASW), 7, 141
  ethics, 143
National Organization for Human
  Services (NOHS), 1, 7, 54, 94,
  127
  ethical standards for human ser-
    vices professionals, 129–134
negative emotions and experiences,
  managing, 35
noncredit internship, 66
noncredit service and learning trips,
  53–54
notes, 108

O

Occupational Outlook Handbook (OOH), 15–16
OCEAN acronym, 30
O*NET Online, 13–15
    skills lists, 14
    Work Values, 14–15
online career and self-knowledge tests and tools, 149–150
online resources, 17
Oregon law, 6
OutOfService, 30

P

paraprofessional activities, 1
paraprofessional jobs, 3
PAR's RIASEC Theory, 16
Peace Corps, 13
peers, 43–44, 54
personality tests, 20
physical well-being, 34
placements. *see also* site placements
    cooperative education, 41, 45
    field, 47–48
    international field, 66
    job-based site placement strategy, 48
postdegree international internship, 67
potential obstacles to employment, 55–56
practicum, 41, 45
prerequisites, 41
primary care medical settings, 2
professional competencies, 41
professional email address, 100
professional ethics
    comparison with human services ethics, 7
    importance of, 9
    structure of, 7–8
professionalism, 45
professional knowledge and skills, 12
professional organizations and conferences, 54
professional portfolio, 56–57, 105
professional presentation, 44–45
professionals in training, 6
program accreditation, 40
program handbook, 39–40
program-wide workshop, 18
public presence, 56

Q

Qualified Mental Health Associate (QMHA), 40, 117

R

reference letters, 106
resources
    campus, 18
    faculty as, 52
    fellow students as, 52
    for cover letters, 104–105
    for job search, 91–92
    for students, 42
    institutional, 39–45
    O*NET, 14
    online, 17
    staff as, 52
    supervisors as, 52
resume, 112
    accuracy and honesty in, 102
    content of, 97
    format and ways of describing experiences, 100
    master copy, 99–100
    presentation listing styles, 101
    professional email address, use of, 100
    templates, 96–97
    tips, 98, 100–103
    utility of, 97–98
    vs curriculum vitae (CV), 57, 96, 98–99

S

scope of practice, 6–7
self-care, 34–35
Self-Directed Search (SDS), 16–17, 61
self-evaluation. *see* career self-evaluation
self-help books, 36
self-promotion, 92–94
service-learning, 41, 45, 66
    experiences, 53
site placements, 45–48, 52
    field exploration using, 51
    supervised site placement experience, 52–53
social work (BSW), 3, 7
specialized roles
    in research and similar settings, 65–66
    international positions, 66
student membership, 95
Substance Abuse and Mental Health Services Administration (SAMHSA), 34
supervision, 11
    campus, 11
    field site, 11
    job, 11

T

Tau Upsilon Alpha National Organization for Human Services Honor Society (TUA), 54
The Balance Careers, 17
The Muse, 17
Three Good Things program, 35
tips
    constructing resume or CV, 100–103
    for avoiding job application errors and problems, 118–119
transference, 31–33
    in long-term therapy relationship, 33
triggers, 31

V

VocBio Vocational Biographies, 68
vulnerabilities, 31

W

What Color Is Your Parachute? 2019: A Practical Manual for Job-Hunters and Career-Changers, 91
Why Zebras Don't Get Ulcers (Robert M. Sapolsky), 35
Workbloom Human Services Resume, 105
workplace restructuring, 59

Y

YES, MAYBE, NO activity, 51

About the Author

Shoshana D. Kerewsky, PsyD, HS–BCP, is a faculty member at the University of Oregon in the Counseling Psychology and Human Services Department and teaches in Clark Honors College as well. A past president of the Oregon Psychological Association, she has helped develop and revise national professional ethics codes and state and national credentialing examinations. She edited *Fitness for the Human Services Profession* for the Council for Standards in Human Service Education (CSHSE) and currently edits the Oregon Psychological Association's quarterly newsletter. As a child, her career goal was to be an astronaut, although by middle school she had decided to become a psychologist.